You've Earned Your Doctorate in Psychology... Now What?

You've Earned Your Doctorate in Psychology… Now What?

Securing a Job as an Academic or Professional Psychologist

**Elizabeth M. Morgan and
R. Eric Landrum**

American Psychological Association • Washington, DC

Published by
American Psychological Association
750 First Street, NE
Washington, DC 20002
www.apa.org

To order
APA Order Department
P.O. Box 92984
Washington, DC 20090-2984
Tel: (800) 374-2721; Direct: (202) 336-5510
Fax: (202) 336-5502; TDD/TTY: (202) 336-6123
Online: www.apa.org/pubs/books
E-mail: order@apa.org

In the U.K., Europe, Africa, and the Middle East, copies may be ordered from
American Psychological Association
3 Henrietta Street
Covent Garden, London
WC2E 8LU England

Typeset in Meridien by Circle Graphics, Inc., Columbia, MD

Printer: Edwards Brothers, Ann Arbor, MI
Cover Designer: Naylor Design, Washington, DC

The opinions and statements published are the responsibility of the authors, and such opinions and statements do not necessarily represent the policies of the American Psychological Association.

Library of Congress Cataloging-in-Publication Data

Morgan, Elizabeth M. (Elizabeth Marie), 1979-
 You've earned your doctorate in psychology— now what? : securing a job as an academic or professional psychologist / Elizabeth M. Morgan and R. Eric Landrum. — 1st ed.
   p. cm.
 Includes bibliographical references and index.
 ISBN 978-1-4338-1145-6 — ISBN 1-4338-1145-6 1. Psychology—Vocational guidance.
 2. Psychology—Study and teaching (Higher) 3. Psychologists. I. Landrum, R. Eric. II. Title.

BF76.M675 2012
150.23—dc23

                                    2011044575

British Library Cataloguing-in-Publication Data
A CIP record is available from the British Library.

Printed in the United States of America
First Edition

Contents

3

4

5

6

7

8

Preface

During the fall of 2008, we were in the midst of telephone interviewing sessions with numerous candidates for a psychology faculty position, each starting every half hour. Some of the applicants were excellent over the telephone, whereas others barely made it through the structured interview questions. Somewhere in the middle of this marathon session, we noted a lack of adequate preparation by many of the candidates, and the idea for this book began to crystallize. The idea led to conversations about the enormous pressures that graduate faculty members are under to teach and to prepare their students to be researchers; sometimes, professional preparation (i.e., preparing for job interviews) is just not part of that curriculum or that mentor's skill set. As a result, there is an obvious need for resources for new psychology doctorates, and we were determined to create a resource. Conversations lead to literature searches about available empirical advice, which lead to outlines, which lead to a book prospectus and our acquisitions editor at American Psychological Association (APA) Books. We wrote this volume to give new psychology doctorates the information and tools they need to get a job.

Elizabeth Morgan arrived at Boise State in August 2008 to be an assistant professor of psychology. In her first semester on the job, she began serving as a member of the departmental search committee. It was handy that during Elizabeth's own job search, she recorded all the questions she was ever asked during telephone and on-site interviews and she kept the itineraries of all of her campus visits. She also talked to her colleagues about their application experiences and job interviews and asked them about their experiences. She was interested in the entire job search process not out of self-interest alone but also because it ignited so many possible lines of scientific inquiry.

Eric Landrum arrived at Boise State in August 1992 and has participated in a departmental search for almost every year since. After reviewing hundreds of curricula vitae, personal statements, teaching portfolios, reprints, and preprints for 20 years, he began to form learned opinions about what a competitive application package comprises. Why do some candidates make such obvious mistakes in their application materials? Why are (some) new doctorates not being mentored better regarding these professional issues? Attention to detail, such as getting the name of our university correct on the cover letter, is important in the job search process. Eric conducted a national study of departmental search committees (Landrum & Clump, 2004) to better understand and advise academic job seekers, and that effort was an important ingredient in fueling his current interest in the job search process.

As always, we are indebted to Linda Malnasi McCarter and the APA editorial team for seeing value in our project and believing that we could complete it in an efficient and effective manner. Editors and authors do not always have trouble-free relationships, but this one is exemplary. It is a real pleasure to work hard for a publisher when the authors know that the publisher will work hard to make the book a success and achieve the ultimate goal: to help new doctorates find meaningful and gainful employment. We thank Linda for her belief in us and in our work. The APA editorial team is also impressive: editorial assistant Jessica Kamish, development editor Susan Herman, and production editor Edward Porter. Many colleagues from around the country shared materials or personal stories with us, and those vignettes help bring our ideas to life. Those colleagues include Matt Genuchi, Boise State University; Jennifer Weaver, Boise State University; Alexandra Dunn, Research Into Action; Sarah Heavin, licensed clinical psychologist; Russell Toomey, Arizona State University; Jessica Irons, James Madison University; and members of the PsychTeacher listserv group.

You've Earned Your Doctorate in Psychology... Now What?

Introduction

Receiving your doctoral degree in psychology (PhD, PsyD, or EdD) is an exercise in delayed gratification. Think about a student—we will call her Jan—who graduates from high school when she is around 18 years old. She attends a fine undergraduate institution and graduates in 4 to 6 years, when she is 22 to 24 years old. If she goes straight from her undergraduate program into a doctoral psychology program, she may finish in 4 to 8 years, depending on the program, specialization, and credentialing. This makes Jan anywhere from 26 to 32 years old when she is faced with the transition from a successful graduate school experience into a successful career—the point at which the long-delayed gratification is (hopefully) delivered. This book is specifically targeted to help new doctorates in psychology make this particular transition: the transition from graduate education to a career in an academic or professional setting.

Even if you have had more changes in your life than Jan has had thus far, such as starting a family, working full time, traveling, or serving in the military, we hope that this book gives you the information and tools you need to make the transition from graduate work to the workforce. In it we use three main strategies, which we describe next.

Evidence-Based Job Advice

There is often a body of scholarly literature that accompanies any topic you could imagine, including the academic and professional job search for doctorates in psychology. Whenever possible, we provide evidence-based advice throughout this book. That is, we provide scholarly and relevant references to empirically based work. When possible, we make our recommendations based on best practices. In addition, we offer real-world experiences where applicable; you will find first person vignettes (narratives) in key locations throughout the book so that you can also "hear" relevant advice from others "in their own words." We call this feature "From the Trenches."

Templates for Job Applications, Cover Letters, Résumés, and the Like

Wherever possible, in addition to sharing our advice, we share actual sample materials as well. We provide examples that show how a cover letter for an academic position might differ from a cover letter for a professional position. The curriculum vitae (CV) for a tenure-track job can differ substantially from a résumé prepared for a professional position such as that of a clinical psychologist joining a practice or an industrial and organizational psychologist heading a human resources department. Not only do we provide evidence-based advice, but we also provide templates and mock-ups of what these documents should look like. By providing you with realistic samples, you will not have to create these documents yourself for your job search—we have done a bit of the heavy lifting for you. We encourage you to seek out examples from your peers who have successfully obtained gainful employment, as well as browse other online and print resources for samples. To this end, we also share with you the best websites, books, and other resources you may want to explore.

Academic Versus Professional

We differentiate *academic* from *professional* jobs using the labeling conventions throughout this volume. When we discuss academic jobs or search strategies for academics, we are addressing the process of seeking a job in the higher education industry—typically a tenure-track assistant professor position. When we discuss professional jobs or search strategies for professionals, we are addressing all of the other employment opportunities outside of higher education. As you will see, this professional side encompasses a wide array of positions, including staff counselor at a health and welfare agency, neuropsychologist conducting research in a hospital setting, or environmental psychologist working for a nonprofit agency. Please understand that we use these terms in reference to a place of employment, not the job duties at hand. Certainly, academics act professionally, and professionals have academic interests. For our purposes, "academic" means working at a university, typically seeking employment as a tenure-track assistant professor, and "professional" means working in nonacademic settings—often more "applied" settings. We use these labels to communicate to you potential work settings, and we emphasize the different job-search strategies based on the setting. Frequently, one size does not fit all.

How to Make the Most of This Book

The goal of this book is provide helpful, specific advice to aid in the transition from your doctoral position and role at your current institution to your new workplace, whether that be in an academic setting or a professional (applied) setting. Chapter 1 offers you a sketch of who today's new doctorates in psychology are and the evolving environment of higher education, where many of them will go on to work. Here you also get a glimpse of the wide variety of job settings for psychology doctorates outside academia. Chapter 2 is about the cover letter, taking you step by step through the process of constructing your own cover letter. Customization is key, and one letter approach does not fit all, especially if you are considering the difference between academic positions and professional positions. In Chapter 3, the CV takes center stage, with precise tips about organization and content and the goal of helping you prepare the most effective CV that you can. Chapter 4 focuses on additional key documents, especially in regard to the search for academic positions. Here you are provided with background information about and key examples of research statements and teaching statements to assist you in preparing your overall portfolio.

Chapter 5 addresses the strategies to use to acquire strong letters of recommendation, including how to build mentoring relationships over time, information to provide letter writers, follow-up, and advice on how to handle difficult situations, should they arise. If all goes well in your job search, preparing for the off-site (screening) interview is the next step in the process. Chapter 6 provides preparation for phone interviews and video interviews, focusing on the types of interview questions likely to be asked for both academic and professional positions. Chapter 7 addresses the key details in an on-site interview, where you are asked to visit the campus, the practice, the organization, or wherever the potential new employer is located. Pre-travel preparations as well as how to deal with illegal interview questions are features of this chapter. Finally, Chapter 8 concludes with a comprehensive planning guide to prepare for success in seeking a job with your doctoral degree—what you do and plan for in graduate school can help to smooth the transition to your next career stop. The Appendix also provides information on negotiating job offers. Where appropriate throughout the chapters, key features will be found in boxes or under special headings that we use to announce their presence.

WHAT THE LITERATURE SAYS . . .

As part of our evidence-based approach, we provide you with empirical findings where they exist. As appropriate, we call your attention to particularly meaningful works in exhibits titled "What the literature says . . ."

FIRST-PERSON VIGNETTES: FROM THE TRENCHES

Different people respond to advice in different ways. Sometimes, personal stories that exemplify life lessons provide meaningful and practical reminders of advice to be followed. Throughout this volume, employers of psychology doctorates share their advice about the application process. As a result, you are able to read brief first-person narratives from those who recently completed a successful academic or professional search, and you hear from folks on the "other side" of the equation—members of search committees and academic departments doing the hiring. Thus, we can offer practical "dos and don'ts" based on real-life experiences of those most directly involved in the hiring process.

THE BOTTOM LINE: TOP RECOMMENDATIONS FOR NEW DOCTORATES

We conclude each of the remaining chapters with a quick summary and recap of the lessons from each chapter. These recommendations are geared to provide you with the best, most comprehensive advice available to date to help with your particular search process. This is where you will find the best nuggets from each chapter in this book. Now let us get to work!

Seeing the Entire Playing Field
Workforce Trends

1

n this chapter, we begin with a review of the career opportunities available to those with a doctorate in psychology, to help you consider whether to pursue an academic or professional position. The available data suggest that either route has positive prospects (Gaugler, 2004). Of the top 25 careers rated in 2009 by *Money* magazine on the basis of average salary, stress level, expected rate of growth, and creativity, college professor was ranked third, and clinical psychologist was ranked 23rd (American Psychological Association [APA], 2009). Career paths for doctors of psychology inside and outside the university context are changing all the time. For this reason, we also discuss networking in this chapter. You may think that networking is something you do to oil the gears in your job search machine once you become a candidate (and we do cover this aspect of networking in Chapter 8 and throughout the volume), but in this chapter we discuss the importance of networking for understanding existing career opportunities, so you can make an informed choice.

What Are the Most Popular Doctoral Degrees in Psychology?

In the last 10 years for which data are available, there has been only a small amount of variability in the number of doctoral degrees in psychology granted in the United States (Snyder & Dillow, 2011; see Table 1.1—for comparison, we include bachelor's degree and master's degree recipients as well). In 2008–2009, the last year for which the data are available, there were 5,477 doctoral degrees in psychology awarded (Snyder & Dillow, 2011). Using APA data to compare these numbers over time (with 2008 as the last year), it is evident that the number of PhDs awarded has remained relatively flat, whereas the number of PsyDs is on the rise (Mulvey & Grus, 2010). Moreover, when the number of clinical PhDs is compared with the number of PsyDs, the number of PsyDs is larger (Mulvey & Grus, 2010).

Table 1.2 shows that those with PhDs in psychology tend to enjoy steady employment, with only 0.8% being unemployed and seeking employment (Michalski & Pate, 2010). Although many of these PhDs enter academic careers, it is important to remember that many PhDs are clinicians, counselors, school psychologists, and other professionals, so the avenues for employment are quite variable. For PsyDs, the employment picture is similar: About 0.7% of PsyDs are unemployed and seeking employment (Michalski & Pate, 2010).

TABLE 1.1

Psychology Degree Recipients, 2003–2009

Year	Psychology degree awarded		
	Bachelor's	Master's	Doctorate
2003–2004	82,098	17,898	4,827
2004–2005	85,614	18,830	5,106
2005–2006	88,134	19,770	4,921
2006–2007	90,039	21,037	5,153
2007–2008	92,587	21,431	5,296
2008–2009	94,271	23,415	5,477
Increase from 2003–2004 to 2008–2009	14.8%	30.8%	13.5%

Note. Adapted from "Digest of Education Statistics 2010" (NCES Report No. 2010-015, Table 326) by T. D. Snyder and S. A. Dillow, 2011, National Center for Education Statistics, Institute of Education Sciences, U.S. Department of Education. Report in public domain.

TABLE 1.2

Employment Characteristics for PhDs and PsyDs

Employment status	Psychology doctorates	
	Psychology PhDs (2006)	Psychology PsyDs* (2008)
% Employed	89.4	97.2
Full-time	68.8	71.4
Part-time	20.6	18.7
% Not Employed	10.6	2.8
Retired	7.8	1.2
Unemployed, seeking employment	0.8	0.7
Unemployed, not seeking employment	2.0	0.9

Note. Data from Michalski and Pate (2010).
*There were also 3.3% enrolled in postdoctoral study for PsyDs. For PhDs, those data are reported separately by the American Psychological Association.

Finding an Academic Career in an Educational Institution

It is typical for graduates to picture a successful career in academia as a tenure-track faculty position within a psychology department at an educational institution. However, not all psychology PhDs are so employed. Psychologists work in schools of education, business, and public health, to name a few. Furthermore, the roles of psychology PhDs within academia can be highly variable as well and are usually dependent on the type of institution (e.g., community college, small private or public college, large public or private university with both undergraduate and graduate education) or the title of the position (e.g., instructor, lecturer, visiting professor, adjunct professor, tenure-track professor). Psychologists may also be hired in research assistant or associate

---

From the Trenches—Applicant Experiences and Advice

I came from a clinically focused doctoral program that did not provide much information or training for careers in academia. Most of what I had learned was from a few close mentors and my spouse.
—Assistant professor and practicing therapist in the Midwest with PhD in child clinical psychology

positions at academic institutions or affiliated research institutes; these positions may be more like professional than academic positions.

The literature available on the academic career paths of psychology PhDs is relatively sparse, as you will see in this chapter and throughout the book. The available information varies from general advice to departmental or career center initiatives to studies of graduate students applying for jobs (rare) to studies of departmental search committees. Although there are some resources available to help new PhD graduates find employment, there are almost no studies specific to psychology that examine the preparation of graduate students for academic careers. One notable exception is the work by Meyers, Reid, and Quina (1998), who found that there were significant gaps in graduate students' training in five academic areas: classroom management, academic life, ethical issues, psychology content, and research training, despite their professional importance. Thus, by using the materials in this book to your advantage, you have the opportunity to be "ahead" of others also pursuing a job with their doctoral degree.

The lack of confidence in one's academic skills, as evidenced by the findings of Meyers et al. (1998), may also be apparent when examining the criteria that departmental search committees consider and value. There appears to be a mismatch between what departmental search committees desire in an applicant and the level of professionalization and job preparation of graduate students. Fortunately, there are studies of departmental admission committee processes (Brems, Lampman, & Johnson, 1995; Landrum & Clump, 2004; Sheehan & Haselhorst, 1999; Sheehan, McDevitt, & Ross, 1998), which offer practical advice, such as the specific recommendations made by Brems et al. (1995) on the basis of their review of actual application materials. Landrum and Clump (2004) reported that evaluative criteria may vary depending on the type of institution (public or private) and type of department (undergraduate-only or undergraduate plus graduate program). In a study specific to the hiring of a social psychologist for an academic position, Sheehan and Haselhorst (1999) concluded the following:

> Although the candidate who was finally selected obviously performed quite well during his visit to campus (at interviews, colloquium, and undergraduate lecture), it was his application materials (vitae, application letter, letters of recommendation, and course evaluations) that first drew him and the other finalists to the attention of the selection committee. (p. 29)

One of the goals of this book is to provide detailed advice, recommendations, and templates to assist you in drawing this type of desired attention to your application materials.

Although their results are difficult to document, there are training programs in existence that work to prepare new doctorates for gainful employment in either academic or professional fields. For example, many doctoral candidates in psychology benefit from the nationwide Preparing Future Faculty (PFF) program offered by the APA (2011). This multidisciplinary program was initiated by the Council of Graduate Schools and the Association of American Colleges and Universities in 1993 (Cook, Kaplan, Nidiffer, & Wright, 2001; Preparing Future Faculty, n.d.) and has evolved into a four-phase program that has been implemented in many different psychology departments in the United States (APA, 2011). If you have a chance to participate in PFF programming, either through institutional involvement or workshops at regional or national conferences, we recommend doing so.

The Division of Geriatrics at the University of Rochester offers an academic career development course that helps students establish competencies using a clinician–teacher–scholar model (Medina-Walpole, Fonzi, & Katz, 2007). By mapping the core competency goals of the course onto objectives of the Accreditation Council for Graduate Medical Education, students achieve competencies in clinical skills, teaching skills, and scholarly skills. This broad approach should be helpful to students; a targeted career development course helps to ensure that all graduate students are exposed to the key elements of a successful graduate student transition from college to career. If these types of programs were more prevalent, perhaps resources such as the one you are reading would not be necessary, but alas, it appears that few career development courses exist at the graduate level in psychology.

Expanding Opportunities in Professional Careers

We should note from the outset that many recipients of PhDs take the professional career route (i.e., nonacademic, applied subfields; Matthews, 2000; Smallwood, 2001), whereas some PsyD recipients enter academia. The type of degree does not define the job setting. Both PhDs and PsyDs work in both types of job setting (Mulvey & Grus, 2010), including universities, 4-year colleges, medical schools, other academic settings, schools and other educational settings, independent practice, hospitals, other human services organizations, managed care, business, government, think tanks, national institutes, consulting companies, and other corporate settings.

There is good advice available for those seeking a career in professional psychology (Hodges & Connelly, 2010; Lopez & Prosser, 2000; Plante, 1998; see Exhibit 1.1), but most of the published advice tends to focus on clinical and counseling psychology positions and not as much on other professional fields, such as school psychology, industrial and

---

EXHIBIT 1.1

Resources for Finding Professional Jobs

- *www.jobrapido.com*—Job listing aggregator that allows for searches in specific subfields, locations, and a radius of opportunities from a location. Use PhD psychology or PsyD psychology in the "What?" box. Users can elect to receive email alerts when new jobs are posted that match their interests.
- *www.ihirementalhealth.com*—Mental health job opportunities organized by job title and by state. Jobs are searchable by state and salary range.
- *www.socialpsychology.org/career.htm#listings*—A listing of multiple resources for job opportunities for both academic and professional in psychology.
- *www.apa.org/careers/psyccareers*—American Psychological Association site providing job listing services for job seekers and employers. Job seekers can establish an account and post a resume here.

---

organizational psychology, or forensic psychology. Two notable exceptions include a book by Basalla and Debelius (2007), which provides a general orientation to choosing, identifying, and getting a professional job, and Sternberg's (2006) collection of essays that review professional career options beyond clinical and counseling psychology, including community psychology, governmental positions, consumer psychology, human factors psychology, military psychology, and health psychology. Within each of these positions there are usually options to engage in professional consultation, supervision, administration, research, teaching or training, and practice.

In looking at current data specific to counseling psychology, the future appears bright. The occupational outlook indicates that counseling fields are expected to grow much faster than average through the year 2016 (Hodges & Connelly, 2010). O*NET (http://www.online. onetcenter.org) offers detailed information about specific professional careers in psychology. By using the tools there, such as "Crosswalks," you can link to other data made available by the U.S. Department of Labor.

Identifying Your Options for Academic and Professional Positions

It is useful to begin identifying your options for academic and non-academic positions as early as possible, because the qualifications that are desirable to your future employer will depend on the type of employment you seek. In addition to reviewing some of the resources we have already discussed, you can further explore these options by browsing job advertisements in the *Chronicle of Higher Education* (http://chronicle.com/section/Home/5) or *Inside Higher Ed* (http://www.insidehighered.com/) and those listed by discipline-specific organizations, such as the APA (http://www.apa.org/) or the Association for Psychological Science (http://www.psychologicalscience.org/).

There are a few books, such as Sternberg's (2006) *Career Paths in Psychology,* that can also be useful for identifying the career possibilities for those with an advanced degree in psychology. Recognizing the variety of positions that exist might help you make some decisions about what types of jobs best match your skills and interests. Knowing that "fit" is one of the most important characteristics employers seek in candidates (e.g., Burns & Kinkade, 2008; Landrum & Clump, 2004), making a preliminary assessment of your own fit with the various options available, and reassessing as necessary, is extremely important.

There are a number of factors to consider in deciding what career route might be the best fit for you. It is likely that you will need to engage in some self-reflection to identify which career path best suits your personality, intellectual interests, and values; there are important differences in duties, schedules, pay, competition, and levels of independence between (and among) the academic and professional spheres. It is also important to realize that there is great diversity within both domains; the type of organization or institution will largely determine the characteristics of the job—and it should similarly determine the characteristics of your application portfolio for that position. For example, community colleges have very different teaching and research requirements and resources than research-oriented universities. Similarly, the National Institutes of Health has a different work culture than a small private think tank. Although you need not select an academic or professional route early on, it is important to be aware of what is available and have an idea of what experiences will make you desirable

---

From the Trenches—Employer Experiences and Advice

The main thing is to work one's network. It's sad to say that the field is an "old boys network," but sometimes it is, and if your mentor/chair/professor knows someone at that institution, a good word from them as a trusted recommendation (vs. one where we don't know the recommender at all) will go a very long ways. Also, go back and exploit all those connections you made at conferences along the way to see if they can give you an "inside scoop" of what the department is like before you step in for interviews. You don't want to make an off-hand comment about how you don't like a particular theory only to find that the department chair loves that theory. Awkward.

—Jennifer R., PhD in clinical psychology, professor and department chair at private religious college in Virginia

for those positions. It is important as well to be aware of the variability within those two routes (e.g., research-oriented vs. teaching-oriented academic positions).

How Networking Can Help You Gather Career Information

In the age of social networking and digital communication, networking is critically important (Plante, 1998). Communicating with others face-to-face or via electronic media or telephone provides key opportunities to seek out career information and to keep informed about job openings and advancement opportunities. Chapter 8 goes more into depth on networking strategies for job candidates; here, we focus on how to create and use your network when your primary purpose is to learn what it is like to work in a particular academic or professional field. Academic advisors are often good at helping you to become a better practitioner or accomplished researcher, but they may not have much expertise in current job search practices. Instead, consider asking the advice of colleagues who graduated a year or two ahead of you and who have already successfully launched their new careers. You may have connections at different universities who share your research or practice interests and whom you should stay in contact with.

Within the large structure of the APA, there are over 50 specialized divisions that are thematically centered on one or another particular aspect of psychology. Divisional membership might also give you another avenue to network with others who share similar interests and who may also be aware of job and career opportunities as they arise. Also, be sure to make use of Listserv and social networking options such as LinkedIn (http://www.linkedin.com). Networking involves the investment of time in others in the hope that by investing in others, you reap benefits as well.

Taking Your Cover Letter to the Next Level

2

T here is a plethora of sources that offer advice on how to prepare a cover letter. For instance, a search on "cover letter" in Google produces over 74 million results within 0.1 seconds. However, this vast quantity of advice is aimed at a general audience and is frequently repetitious. In this chapter, we offer specific advice about writing cover letters in application for academic or professional doctoral positions.

Make Each Part of the Cover Letter Count

If you read enough about the preparation and formatting of cover letters, some helpful broad-based advice does tend to emerge. The typical cover letter has four different

---

From the Trenches—Employer Experiences and Advice

The cover letter is the most important item. It sets the tone for the rest of the materials. If it stinks, we frequently go no further.
—Kelly J., PhD in social psychology, assistant professor at a private college in the Northeast

---

components: the salutation, the opening paragraph, the body, and the conclusion (Crosby, 1999; Jenkins, 2010). We discuss each of these components in turn, with advice to make them look polished.

SALUTATION

Do everything possible to address your cover letter to a specific person. It might require a little digging or research to avoid potential social blunders, such as addressing your letter to "Dear Sirs" or "To Whom It May Concern." If there is a person listed as a contact in the job posting, be sure to find out who that person is so you can address him or her appropriately (e.g., chair of the department, chair of the search committee, administrative assistant). If there is not a specific person listed as the contact person or chair of the search committee, find out the name of the appropriate person. This may be the occasion to use your network of contacts to determine the specific person to write to. This detail could help you stand out from a crowd of applicants. First, a letter addressed to a specific person is more direct and easier to write (in our opinion) than a generic letter. Second, by finding out who the key person in the search committee is when that person was not listed in the job advertisement indicates that you are willing to do your homework on the organization or institution to which you are applying. However, if after all your sleuthing you cannot find the name of a specific contact person, an appropriate alternative is to address the letter to the "Chair of the Search Committee."

OPENING PARAGRAPH

The opening paragraph is absolutely key: You must be completely accurate but also grab the reader's attention. Rather than starting with the traditional restatement of the position being applied for (save that for

---

From the Trenches—Employer Experiences and Advice

Make it 100% clear why you are drawn to a particular institution in the cover letter. We are looking for people who will actually come and be excited to join us. Make it seem like you want to be a part of us. In the cover letter include information about *why* that specific school. Are you interested in a liberal arts college? The region? Particular people to collaborate with? Sometimes people have the wrong names or information. If you are applying to the University of Blah Blah, make sure all of your documents match that.

—Eleni P., PhD in cognitive psychology, assistant professor at a small public liberal arts college

the last sentence of the opening paragraph), start with a statement that demonstrates both your personal appeal as well as those credentials that distinguish you from other applicants. Your first statement should be an attention grabber—something that will make the reader want to read the second sentence and beyond. Imagine 200 applicants, all with doctorates in psychology, applying for one clinical position or one faculty position. Almost every applicant will begin with a statement almost identical to the following: "I am writing to apply for your department's tenure-track assistant professor position in psychology." Instead, think about what trait, quality, characteristic, or experience helps you to stand out from the crowd (e.g., "My expertise in the social and cultural contexts of children's cognitive development and experience with community-based research uniquely qualifies me for your Assistant Professor position.") This is what should be highlighted in your first paragraph.

When you do mention the position you are applying for, be sure that all the details are correct. If the department has a position available for a tenure-track assistant professor in cognitive psychology, do not end your opening paragraph by saying that you are pleased to be applying to for the open position in social psychology. Similarly, if you are applying to become the director of clinical training at Idaho State University, do not state in your cover letter that you look forward to meeting the challenges at Boise State University (these are distinctly different schools). These mix-ups do actually happen and can result in instant rejection without examination of any other applicant materials.

BODY

It is in the body of your cover letter that you get the chance to explain how your qualifications match the job description (Crosby, 1999). It is best to address the job requirements directly: If the job advertisement emphasizes the completion of clinical hours, then address this in the cover letter by stating when the hours were completed (and better yet, when the license was issued) or when the hours will be completed, listing a specific month. Different paragraphs of the cover letter should emphasize different aspects of the job, such as teaching and research. Regardless, be sure to customize each letter to precisely address the job qualifications of each position (Thompson, 2009); this will likely require more research on the department and institution than simply reviewing the job advertisement. As you review the body of the cover letter, make sure each sentence is vital to the message or story you are telling—if you can remove a sentence without changing the intent or message, then remove it. In addition to all the other functions it serves, the cover letter is also a sample of your writing and clarity of thought.

CONCLUSION

The conclusion is where you get the chance to show your commitment to the position (Crosby, 1999). Make sure that your interest in that particular position is adequately conveyed (which will involve more customization than simply pasting in the name of the school), and review your interests, experiences, and training that relate to the specific position you are applying for. Provide the details needed for you to be reached easily, and last, make the *ask*. In the fundraising world (or in sales), the ask is the point at which you ask for the action you wish to receive—in fundraising, for example, the ask is about making a specific donation. As an applicant, be sure to make the ask for the next step (Jenkins, 2010)—whether that be a telephone interview; an on-site interview at the clinic, business, hospital, or department; or an interview using Skype, for example. Depending on your personality, this behavior might seem a bit forward, but you want to be seen as enthusiastic and excited about the next steps of the application process. Given that none of us make a career of continuously applying for jobs, there are times when we are pushed out of our comfort zone—this book should help you with strategies to navigate these processes and work to minimize those discomforts as much as possible.

The Cover Letter Dissected: Length, Level of Detail, Personal Disclosure, and Presentation

In the resources we review here and later in the chapter, there is conflicting advice about the preferred length of a cover letter for those who have received new doctorates. Woolf (2010) and Durand (2011) both recommended that a good cover letter fit on two double-spaced pages (or one single-spaced page). As Jenkins (2010) suggested, the cover letter is typically the potential employer's first impression of you, so it matters greatly (although he hedges on length: at least one page long, but no longer than two). Note that some of the sample job advertisements presented in Exhibit 2.1 specifically call for a cover letter, whereas others ask for statements that will consist of some or all parts of a cover letter.

Take your cues about what to include in your cover letter from the job advertisement (or better yet, from someone you know in the hiring unit or department). If the job announcement is detailed and specifically

EXHIBIT 2.1

Sample Job Advertisements for Professional and Academic Positions

---

Professional Positions

1. Step into a thriving private practice with a well-appointed office and a full caseload of mainly professional and business people, as well as complete support services, including billing and collection. An established private psychology practice is looking for a Florida licensed or license-eligible psychologist with experience and training evaluating and treating children and families (both intact, divorcing and divorced) with skills in marital and family therapy, as well as adult psychotherapy. Other desirable expertise includes psycho-educational or neuropsychological testing, parenting (custody), or forensic evaluations. Strong writing skills appreciated. The center has served Southwest Florida for 33 years and is a growing, non–managed care practice. Successful applicants will be offered the opportunity to become a shareholder/partner. Send letter of interest, curriculum vitae, and sample report to human resources by e-mail to humanresources@fakeprivatepractice.com or fax to (555) 936-1234.

2. THE POSITION: Located in either or Boston-area or Kansas City-area offices, a leading learning research organization is expanding our team by hiring nine fulltime, permanent Lead Researchers (PhD level) and Research Associates (MS level). These positions will have responsibility for assisting with numerous large-scale research initiatives designed to inform and drive new learning related product development as well as product modification. Specifically, the Lead Researchers and Research Associates will provide assistance throughout the studies; conducting extensive literature reviews, monitoring implementation and data collection procedures, analyzing data, and production of the final report and recommendations.

   REQUIRED CANDIDATE EXPERIENCE & QUALIFICATIONS: Excellent written and verbal communication skills, ability to tailor to a broad spectrum of stakeholders; a PhD or Master's in statistics, educational research, or in the business decision sciences area; high level of proficiency with PASW [Predictive Analytics SoftWare] or Excel; strong experience and skills in quantitative research design, data collection, and statistical analysis; outstanding ability to apply search techniques across numerous disciplines and databases; experience working with large datasets; one to three years experience working in a research intensive environment; ability to translate/use data to inform decisions; and a strong track record of publications and presentations a plus.

   To apply, select the "Apply for this Job" button located at the top or bottom of the page.

   Send your resume to: resumes@aresearchcompany.com. We are proud to be an Equal Opportunity Employer. No agency or search firm submissions will be accepted. Applications for U.S. based positions must be legally authorized to work in the United States and verification of employment eligibility will be required at the time of hire. Visa sponsorship is not available for this position.

   NOTES: 9 openings.
   >Additional Salary Information: In addition to market competitive base salary Ascend Learning offers a cash bonus incentive program, health and wellness benefits and 401(K).

Academic Positions

1. A midwestern college invites applications for a tenure track position in psychology with an emphasis in Neuroscience to begin September 1, 2012. The successful candidate will help to initiate and guide our new integrative Neuroscience program. A PhD is required and

(continued)

EXHIBIT 2.1 (*Continued*)

appointment at the assistant professor level is anticipated, though higher ranks may be considered for suitably qualified applicants. Applicants should exhibit a potential for excellence in undergraduate teaching and mentoring, as well as a commitment to scholarship that includes collaborative research with undergraduates. The successful candidate will be expected to teach introductory and junior-level neuroscience courses (with labs), and courses such as General Psychology, Drugs & Behavior, or other courses that match the candidate's expertise. Applicants will have opportunities to contribute to an interdisciplinary general education program. The college, founded in the mid 1800s, is a selective, comprehensive liberal arts college with an enrollment of 2900 students, located in Springfield. See http://www.midwesterncollege.edu for more information about the school and the department. Review of applications will begin on November 3, 2011 and will continue until the position is filled. Applicants should submit a letter of application, curriculum vitae, a statement of teaching interests/philosophy, a statement of research interests and plans, unofficial photocopies of graduate transcripts, and arrange for three letters of recommendation to be sent to: Psychology/Neuroscience Search Committee, c/o Academic Affairs Office, Midwestern College, or e-mail your materials in PDF format to jobsearch@midwesterncollege. edu. Applicants who would enrich the diversity of the campus community are especially encouraged to apply. An Equal Opportunity Employer.

2. A Southern University (SU) invites applications for a tenure-track Assistant Professor position in its Clinical Psychology master's program beginning August 2012. Doctorate in clinical psychology or closely related discipline required. Must show potential for scholarly productivity and enthusiastic teaching, with genuine concern for student achievement. Successful candidate will play central role in clinical training of students. Responsibilities include teaching, research, clinical supervision, mentoring of students, and service to the university and community. Area of specialization is open, with preference given to candidates with interests in one or more of the following: assessment, child clinical, gerontology, multicultural counseling, treatment outcome, or severe and persistent psychopathology. Interest in psychotherapies that complement and expand the program's already strong CBT emphasis is desirable. Preference given for graduation from APA-accredited doctoral program, completion of APA-accredited pre-doctoral internship, psychology licensure or license-eligibility, and contribution to program diversity. SU is a culturally diverse, upper-level university (juniors, seniors, and master's students) adjacent to a NASA space center. Located in the a recreational area, the scenic campus is 30 minutes from downtown, which is home to a large medical center. Applications accepted only online at https://jobs.susu.edu. Review of completed applications begins November 1, 2011 and will continue until position is filled. To apply, complete the online faculty application and include cover letter, curriculum vitae, and submit names and email addresses of three references. These references will be contacted by our automated system and asked to submit a letter online. Proof of eligibility to work in US must be provided. Only applicants selected for further consideration will be contacted. An Affirmative Action/Equal Opportunity Employer supporting workplace diversity. We reserve right to extend search or not fill position.

asks for many pieces of information, then your cover letter will likely be longer so that you can be thorough. If the required information and job advertisement is succinct, then you may want to follow the lead provided. Although there are many pieces of obvious advice offered anywhere you read about cover letters (e.g., no typographical errors, no grammatical errors, crisp black ink on bright white paper if the cover letter is submitted on paper), one perhaps overlooked tidbit comes from Jenkins (2010). He recommended that, whether submitting electronically (as a PDF or e-mail) or on paper, you use a 12-point font, probably Times New Roman: "Remember the middle-aged eyes of the search-committee members" (para. 6).

According to Williams-Nickelson and Prinstein (2007), the amount of background information to disclose in a cover letter is related to one's comfort level; however, some readers believe that "personal disclosures are inappropriate and indicative of loose boundaries" (p. 50). An example of a personal disclosure is: "I want to apply for positions on the East Coast because that is where I grew up, and I am looking forward to returning to that part of the country." Make sure you have your advisor and other trusted mentors review all the materials before you submit your application—these individuals are likely familiar with job application standards and should be able to give you invaluable feedback about your level of self-disclosure and whether your approach in your cover letter (and other materials) should be changed. Exhibit 2.2 provides some additional suggestions to consider when crafting your cover letter.

From the Trenches—Applicant Experiences and Advice

What seemed to work well for me was constructing a vague template and then updating each paragraph with the requisite information. Paragraph one was always a brief introduction, and paragraph two was about why I was interested in the position. Paragraph three was about research, four about teaching, five about service and administrative interests (not everyone will have this), and six was about geography. The statements about myself did not change much from letter to letter, but I spent a lot of time scouring the websites for specific course numbers and titles I might want to teach, features of the program that were attractive to me as a candidate, and features of the geographic region that I found alluring. The template allowed me to write cover letters efficiently, which was important because they were the biggest drain on my time during the application process.

—Jennifer V., PhD in psychology

> **EXHIBIT 2.2**
>
> **What the Literature Says . . . About Impression Management**
>
> Every applicant likely realizes that it is important to "put your best foot forward," but the researchers in the field of impression management have identified specialized tactics for doing so that may be especially well received by potential employers. Varma, Toh, and Pichler (2006) specifically examined *ingratiation* as a method to increase liking or apparent competence in order to appear more employable. They explored four ingratiation tactics and their relative influence on personnel selection decisions (p. 202):
>
> - *Self-enhancement.* The subordinate engages in behavior or conversation aimed at improving his or her image in the mind of the supervisor.
> - *Other-enhancement.* The subordinate attempts to praise the achievements or qualities of the supervisor.
> - *Opinion conformity.* The subordinate attempts to ingratiate him- or herself to the supervisor by agreeing with the supervisor's opinions.
> - *Rendering favors.* The subordinate tries to ingratiate him- or herself to the supervisor by rendering favors beyond the call of work-related duty.
>
> Graduate students ($N = 94$) enrolled in human resources courses were asked to rate five different cover letters: four containing one of each of the types of ingratiation and a control letter without ingratiation. Judgments were made about an applicant's overall qualifications as well as hiring recommendations.
>
> The pattern of results was identical for both the overall qualifications decisions and the hiring recommendations. The cover letter receiving the most positive response was the self-enhancement cover letter. There was a significant difference between it and the next grouping, other-enhancement and opinion conformity cover letters (there was no significant difference between these tactics). There was also a significant difference between the second and the final grouping, rendering favors and no ingratiation (with no difference between these two tactics).
>
> Of course, as Knouse, Giacalone, and Pollard (1988) reported, the tone of the cover letter must be considered in relation to the entire application package. However, Varma et al. (2006) noted that their study only referred to written ingratiation tactics; application procedures over the telephone or in-person interviews may not be subject to the same impression management outcomes. Nevertheless, to the extent that you are comfortable with this approach, writing a cover letter with the specific intent of improving your own image and with these tactics in mind may lead to higher perceptions of your qualifications and ultimately to a hiring recommendation.

Cover Letters for Professional Positions and a Sample Letter

Advice about cover letters offered to job seekers with doctorates in applied psychology (e.g., clinical, counseling, industrial and organizational; Hitchings & Ornellas, 1999; Hodges & Connelly, 2010; Williams-Nickelson & Prinstein, 2007) is not much different from that offered to those seeking academic positions. For example, Hitchings and Ornellas

(1999) recommended that in the cover letter the applicant link relevant clinical experiences to the type of setting listed in the advertisement and provide the status of licensure. Advice about the length of the cover letter differs slightly among authors. Hitchings and Ornellas (1999) suggested no more than one page; Williams-Nickelson and Prinstein (2007) recommended "1 page only, certainly no more than 2 pages" (p. 50); and Hodges and Connelly (2010) contended that if the cover letter is more than three to four paragraphs (or more than one typed page), it is too long.

Williams-Nickelson and Prinstein (2007) reiterated the notion that the cover letter conveys the first impression and that for some reviewing the application package, the cover letter is the most important document. The goals of the cover letter for the new doctor of psychology applying for a professional position include (a) to concisely explain the reasons why he or she is a strong applicant for the position; (b) to share enough background information to create interest and lead the reader to want to know more about the applicant by, for example, reviewing the applicant's résumé or curriculum vitae (CV); and (c) to provide follow-up contact details (Hodges & Connelly, 2010). The sample professional cover letter focuses exclusively on both of these goals. An actual advertisement for a professional position is shown in Exhibit 2.3. The cover letter written in application for this job is shown in Figure 2.1.

Cover Letters for Academic Positions and a Sample Letter

The published literature on cover letters for academic positions seems more sparse and less current than that for applied, professional positions, and it is hard to know why. It could be that cover letters for academic positions are just pro forma documents that literally serve as "covering letters" for all the documents submitted with the job application. However, because it is hard to predict what will be important to a search committee, the cover letter should be treated as a significant part of the application package and carefully crafted to present the application in the best light.

Brems, Lampman, and Johnson (1995) provided valuable information about characteristics of academic applicant cover letters and the pitfalls encountered in crafting them. For example, these researchers reported that the mean length of a cover letter was 40.2 lines ($SD = 29.6$), with a mode and median of 34 lines and a range of four lines to 150 lines. (For context, a single-spaced 8.5 × 11-in. sheet of paper with 1-in. margins contains 54 lines.) In addition, a committee of reviewers who were

EXHIBIT 2.3

Example of a Professional Job Advertisement

State Department of Education
Every Student, Every Day—A Success!

State Superintendent of Public Instruction, Jane Superintendent, and the State Department of Education provide statewide leadership for all elementary and secondary students in the state's public school districts and education service districts. Responsibility also extends to public preschool programs, the state school for the deaf, regional programs for children with disabilities, and education programs in state youth corrections facilities.

This recruitment is to augment the candidate pool generated by job announcement EDUC-0005 and EDUC11-0005A. If you have previously applied for this position, you need not re-apply. Names of qualified applicants will remain on the list for further consideration.

There is currently one permanent, full-time position available with the Office of Assessment and Information Services at the State Department of Education. This position is classified and represented by Service Employees International Union (SEIU).

The Office of Assessment and Information Services has two primary functions: student assessment; and the collection, validation, and reporting of data for education research, policy-making, and operations. The technical expertise of staff in this unit is available to districts to support business and financial functions. The work of OAIS affects every school, program, school district, and education service district (ESD) in the state. Nearly all students in the state public school system are affected by the work in these units. Data is collected from nearly every educational administrative unit.

This recruitment will be used to establish a list of qualified people and may be used to fill vacancies as they occur.

Applicants will be subject to a thorough background investigation including driving record. Adverse background data may be grounds for immediate disqualification. Applicants will be subject to a computerized criminal history check. Conviction of a crime will not automatically preclude an appointment. The circumstances involved in the conviction will be considered.

DUTIES AND RESPONSIBILITIES
The primary purpose of this position is to securely perform data collection, data cleaning, research and analysis in the areas of accountability, school and district staff, student performance, student demographics, and related topics in support of the policy initiatives of the Department of Education. This position will plan and design research studies and conduct analyses necessary to evaluate internal and external policies and programs. In addition, this position will be expected to communicate with stakeholders regarding data quality issues and the results of research studies.

Major duties include:

Research Planning, Design, and Analyses
- Independently plan and conduct major, analytical or statistical research projects related to the state's Education Accountability System and related high stakes accountability data (e.g. high school dropouts, high school graduates, student performance, school and district staff)
- Develop procedures that describe the series of steps to be taken by analysts
- Establish and implement procedures to verify the quality of data and the results of the research projects
- Establish business rules and conduct validation of accountability data
- Ensure security procedures are followed when handling data
- Consult with stakeholders regarding business rules and data collection processes
- Use either Transact-SQL or SPSS to extract, validate, analyze, and report data from various databases and files
- Participate with Information Systems staff in planning, designing and implementing new or enhanced information systems

(continued)

EXHIBIT 2.3 (*Continued*)

Report Preparation
- Review accountability data and reports for clarity and accuracy
- Write statistical and narrative summary reports and articles for publication with audience appropriate language and content that explain the process used to collect the data, how to interpret the results, and implications for the education system
- Produce clear and accurate summary graphs and charts
- Train and guide lower level analysts in report writing

Technical Consultant
- Confer with internal and external stakeholder groups regarding current data, trends, projections, or impact of existing or proposed studies (e.g. ODE management and policy-makers, media, community groups, advisory committees, etc.)
- Prepare written responses, technical expertise and specialized information upon request
- Provide training and assistance to schools and school districts related to data collection, data validation, and the interpretation of results

Project Coordination
- Design research-project methodology and plan, assign, check, and coordinate the work of other accountability and reporting staff
- Provide technical direction for the office including verifying the accuracy, validity and completeness of data and reports generated by other staff
- Lead and coordinate major research projects or survey programs
- Coordinate projects that include broad cross-functional team members

WORKING CONDITIONS
General office environment with extensive use of computers with a variety of software for data management, analysis, and presentation.

QUALIFICATIONS AND DESIRED ATTRIBUTES

Minimum Qualifications
A Bachelor's Degree in any disciplines that included six-quarter units in statistics or quantitative analysis methods and procedures, and three years experience using computerized applications to independently gather, compile, and analyze data and prepare narrative or statistical reports. Two of the three years must have included coordinating complex research projects.

OR

Five years of research experience using computerized applications to independently gather, compile, and analyze data and prepare narrative or statistical reports. Two of the five years must have included coordinating complex research projects.

AND

Experience in using trends such as social, economic, or industrial to do analytical research Experience using advanced statistical or quantitative analysis computer applications College-level course work in advanced statistics or quantitative analysis that includes such methods as multiple regression, factor analysis, analysis of variances, and discriminate analysis.

Desired Attributes
Excellent verbal and written communication, analytic and organizational skills. Statistical software such as SPSS or SAS, relational database management systems language such as SQL, advanced spreadsheet and data base experience required, as well as experience with large complex transactional systems preferred. Experience interpreting, analyzing and implementing state and federal polices into business accountability and research systems.

FIGURE 2.1

Susan Smith, PhD
555 Portland St.
Portland, OR 97202
503-555-0101
youremail@gmail.com

July 1, 2012

Ms. Jane Jones
State Department of Education
255 Capitol Street NE,
State, ST 01254-4411

Dear Ms. Jones:

In response to your job posting on the state.gov website (code: EDUC11-0005B), I am enclosing my resume and unofficial transcripts. I think you will find that my background as a researcher and statistical analyst in academic research, combined with my private industry experience, provides a close match to the criteria mentioned in your advertisement.

I recently finished my doctoral dissertation in psychology at Smart University. During my tenure at Smart University, I created statistical protocols for large research projects as a consultant, and I created my own research agenda from idea to publication. Specifically, I designed a reading literacy scale, conducted international research and data gathering, and used advanced qualitative and quantitative analytical methods to analyze and interpret the data gathered.

To garner private industry experience I also worked with the language testing company Pearson. While at Pearson, I assessed the validity and reliability of an English language test for adults and helped overhaul the English language test for middle school children.

Through my graduate career, I gained more than 7 years of experience creating, executing, analyzing, and authoring complex research projects. To conduct and analyze my research, I led a large group of undergraduate research assistants.

To expand my statistical knowledge, I took advanced graduate-level statistics courses ranging from multivariate techniques to factor analysis. I deepened my statistical knowledge by seeking out teaching assistantships in undergraduate research methods, as well as introductory and advanced statistics courses.

I have used SPSS, JMP, SAS, and R in my research and teaching. In addition, I understand the underlying logic used to create complex relational databases. I have worked with computer programmers to extract and analyze data from large databases.

As you will see from my resume, I am an avid learner, and I am eager to apply the skills I have learned to a new sector. Although my mix of academic and private experience may not initially present an identical mapping to your criteria, I am confident that my analytical and agile thinking can be an ideal match for the State Department of Education. If you should need any additional information, please feel free to call me (503-555-0101) or e-mail me (youremail@gmail.com).

Sincerely,

Susan Smith

Example cover letter for a professional position.

TABLE 2.1

Analysis of Applicants' Cover Letters

Issue to be addressed	% who addressed issue correctly	% who did not address issue or addressed incorrectly
Identify position	89.9	10.1
Courses to be taught	63.7	36.3
Research interests	85.1	14.9
Teaching interests	61.8	38.2
Academic advising	10.1	89.9
Grant experience	23	77.0
Work with culturally diverse students	7.5	92.5
Program development	9.5	90.5
Excessive personal information	9.7	90.3
Excessive detail about research findings	27.1	72.9

Note. Reprinted from "Preparation of Applications for Academic Positions in Psychology," by C. Brems, C. Lampman, and M. E. Johnson, 1995, *American Psychologist, 50*, p. 534. Copyright 1995 by the American Psychological Association.

evaluating actual job applications analyzed cover letters to determine the percentage of applicants who addressed pertinent job information and qualifications. Interrater reliabilities of .9 or better were reached. The surprising results are presented in Table 2.1.

Although these data are a bit dated, it is clear that when applicants do not address (or misaddress) the items listed in the job advertisement, their search committee ratings suffer. When the applicant failed to address the specific advertised position, search committee members gave the applicant a poor rating because it appeared that he or she was not interested enough in the position. It is surprising that such high percentages of applicants did not address some issues at all, or addressed them incorrectly. Many applicants were rated poorly because of their failure to address issues such as their ability to work with culturally diverse students, their program development experience, and their academic advising experience. They were also rated poorly because of their inclusion of excessive personal information and too much detail about research findings.

On the basis of their data and multiple years' experience serving on search committees, Brems et al. (1995) provided some detailed advice for writing the academic cover letter:

- Never submit a generic cover letter.
- Do not make the cover letter less than two pages long.
- Do not include personal information in a cover letter or CV unless it is salient to why you are applying for the position.
- Do not submit applications—and especially cover letters—with typographical, grammatical, or punctuation errors.

> ▪ Always remember to sign your cover letter and provide accurate phone numbers for where you can be reached. (pp. 536–537)

We would like to offer two additional ideas. First, in regard to the last bulleted point, be sure to include your e-mail address in the cover letter, and be sure the address looks professional; if you no longer have access to a university e-mail address ending in .edu, a (free) Gmail account with an appropriate username will suffice. Second, although Brems et al. (1995) suggested that the academic cover letter must be at least two pages long (and perhaps longer), in their own study, the average cover letter length was 40.2 lines on a 54-line page, and the median and modal length was 34 lines. Be sure to rely on your support system (e.g., mentors, graduate faculty) for advice and feedback about all the materials you will be submitting for a doctoral-level job application, including the content and length of your cover letter.

The job advertisement for which our sample cover letter was written is shown in Figure 2.2. Figure 2.3, courtesy of Dr. Matt Genuchi, a newly hired assistant professor of psychology at Boise State University, is an example of how an academic cover letter could be crafted and assembled.

The Bottom Line: Top Recommendations for New Doctorates

From broad-based approaches to finer grained analyses, here are our top recommendations for preparing a cover letter for academic or professional job applications.

MATCH YOUR LETTER TO THE ADVERTISEMENT

Whatever the specific details of the job or jobs you are applying for, make sure that in your cover letter you emphasize that your skills match those called for in the position description. You might have a general template of information that you are using to craft your letters, but make sure that each letter is customized for the position for which you are applying. Attention to detail matters.

Under the pseudonym Clement Vincent, an associate professor who has frequently served on search committees offered a hypothetical rejection letter that he wished could be sent to unsuccessful applicants. The following is an excerpt from that letter:

> In short, if we had to make up a story for why you were interested in our position, then interviewing you was too risky. There

FIGURE 2.2

BOISE STATE UNIVERSITY

ASSISTANT PROFESSOR
PSYCHOLOGY
SS-043107-01

The Department of Psychology at Boise State University (http://sspa.boisestate.edu/psychology) invites applications for a tenure-track assistant professor beginning fall 2011.

Responsibilities:

- Candidates should have the potential for excellence in teaching and demonstrated research productivity.

- Teaching interests should include areas such as Developmental Psychology, Abnormal Psychology, Research Methods, as well as other related courses.

- The preferred candidate will have an interest in participating in the Family Studies Initiative.

- Research interests are open, but an emphasis on some aspect of applied psychology is preferred.

At a minimum, you should have:

Position applicants are required to have an earned doctorate in Psychology or Human Development and Family Studies by August 15, 2011.

If this sounds like the job for you:

Please submit **electronically (PDF)** a cover letter outlining your qualifications and areas of teaching and research interest, curriculum vita, copies of preprints or reprints, teaching and research statements and contact information only for three references to staffsearch@boisestate.edu or mail to:

Faculty Search
Department of Psychology
9999 University Dr.
Boise, ID 83725

Review of applications will begin on November 15, 2010, and will continue until finalists are identified. Applications received after November is will only be considered if the position is not filled from the original finalist pool.

Job advertisement for sample cover letter.

were many other applicants who stated in concrete terms why they wanted to teach on our campus. Here's the moral of all this: Every cover letter should state precisely and persuasively why the applicant is seeking the job. A few of you seemed quite excited about fonts in your applications. I must tell you that wildly underlining and bolding phrases, or occasionally changing the font size for keywords on your cover letters, does not betoken professionalism. When I encountered such letters, it was hard not to hear the intonation of a desperate sales rep trying a bit too hard to close a deal. Additionally, we set aside a few applications

FIGURE 2.3

Faculty Search
Department of Psychology
9999 University Drive
Boise, ID 83725

October 27, 2010

Dear Search Committee Members:

I am writing to apply for the position of assistant professor in psychology beginning in fall 2011, as advertised on your department website. I currently work in full-time clinical practice at Life Counseling Center in Nampa, ID, where I am completing my requirements to become licensed as a psychologist in Idaho. I am extremely interested in obtaining a faculty position at Boise State University because I believe that employment at Boise State will allow me to make a valuable contribution to the university through an established program of scholarship, actively foster learning in and outside of the classroom, and serve the community of Boise.

I believe that my academic training in the APA-accredited counseling psychology program at the University of Denver has provided me with valuable research skills that will allow me to be a productive researcher in the psychology department at BSU. I am passionate about the clinical issues related to the psychology of men and masculinity, and my doctoral dissertation involved use of self-report questionnaires to investigate a model of masculine depression in a sample of male college students. My research interests are not limited to men's issues, though, as I also am actively involved in scholarship by contributing to the conceptualization of a competency-based model of clinical supervision for the fields of clinical and counseling psychology. Furthermore, I have been involved in several collaborative projects investigating clinical supervision competency. My colleagues and I published our first study in the APA's *Training and Education in Professional Psychology*, and in April 2010 we submitted our second study for peer review. We are also in the process of developing additional collaborative research projects, which I believe would be valuable to the psychology department at Boise State.

In addition to scholarship, I am very passionate about teaching and supporting the academic success of students. My commitment to teaching is evidenced by my involvement in teaching undergraduate students as an adjunct faculty member since 2005. As a graduate student, I taught at the Metropolitan State College of Denver, and I currently teach psychology courses at the College of Western Idaho. While I have primarily taught General Psychology courses, my academic training included a broad range of topics in counseling and clinical psychology, which

Example cover letter for an academic position. Copyright 2010 by Matthew C. Genuchi. Printed with permission.

FIGURE 2.3 (*Continued*)

would allow me to teach a broad range of applied psychology courses at Boise State, such as Personality Theory, Introduction to Counseling Skills, General Psychology, Abnormal Psychology, Internship in Psychology, Theories of Psychotherapy and Counseling, and Psychological Measurement.

I also believe in the positive impact that psychological services and knowledge can have on the community. Based on my desire for community involvement, I have worked the past year in a community-based counseling clinic in Nampa, ID, which primarily serves underprivileged families in Canyon County. I have been able to integrate my interests in masculinity with my clinical practice through my work with a large number of children and adolescent boys. I was involved in significantly expanding the scope of the psychological assessment practice area. Through Life Counseling, I have also served as a mental health consultant to two regional Head Start centers, one of which is in Marsing and one of which is in Caldwell.

Because of my research interests in applied psychology, my academic and clinical training in counseling psychology, my passion for engaging instruction, and my belief in the value of community service, I believe that I am an excellent match for the assistant professor position in the Boise State psychology department. For your review I have enclosed my curriculum vitae, teaching statement, research statement, three professional references, and article reprints and preprints. If you require any additional materials or have any questions, please do not hesitate to contact me. Thank you very much for your consideration.

Sincerely,

Matthew C. Genuchi, PhD
123 Elm Street
Garden City, ID 83714
(208) 555-1212

matt.genuchi@fakeemail.com

Example cover letter for an academic position. Copyright 2010 by Matthew C. Genuchi. Printed with permission.

with cover letters that came across as arrogant. One of you stated that you considered yourself to be one of the few instructors in the country qualified to teach in our discipline. We couldn't help wonder how you would feel about your colleagues if we were to hire you. (Vincent, 2008, para. 19–22)

CONSIDER MENTOR FEEDBACK BEFORE YOU SUBMIT YOUR APPLICATION

Your graduate school mentors have much invested in you and want to see you succeed. A good mentor will not only emphasize a particular theoretical research approach or a particular therapeutic orientation but will also happily assist in your job search. Make sure you show your mentor at least a sample of the type of cover letter you intend to send (as well as other documents, such as your CV or résumé, teaching and research statements, teaching portfolios, etc). Give your mentor enough time to carefully review your documents and return them to you, so you can incorporate their suggestions and submit your materials on time. Your mentor can provide specific advice for you, but Sha (2011) offered doctoral students (from all disciplines) this advice regarding cover letters:

- Do not claim credentials or expertise in an area where you possess neither.
- Do not assume that because your theoretical approach or research is interesting to you that it will be inherently interesting to others.
- If you have not completed your dissertation or doctoral project, include your estimated date of completion. The closer you are to completing your dissertation or doctoral projects, the more competitive an applicant you will be.
- Do not provide readers with a list of authors, theories, or theorists that have influenced your particular approach to the field.
- Pay attention to all the details. Proof your letter carefully.

ATTEND TO SUBMISSION DETAILS

It is important to realize that the format used in a hardcopy cover letter will be different from that used in an e-mail. The same four-part structure (salutation, opening paragraph, body, conclusion) may be used, but modified for the medium. Thompson (2009) suggested that for e-mail cover letters, to avoid the jargon and casual tone often used in e-mail. In addition, because the e-mail cover letter may be read on a relatively small mobile phone screen, the body section of the cover letter should contain fewer points than the hardcopy cover letter. Always follow the application instructions precisely, but if possible, you might follow up the e-mail cover letter with a hardcopy version (or PDF attached to an e-mail).

Preparing Your Curriculum Vitae 3

T here is an amazing amount of power in a well-told story; stories can convince us, persuade us, inspire us, humiliate us, and move us to action. Stories are also remarkable memory devices (Simmons, 2006; Willingham, 2009)—just think about your own family stories, stories about summer vacations and undergraduate coursework, the first kiss and the first broken heart, and so on. And although it may not be as dramatic a story, your curriculum vitae (CV) is one of your key storytelling devices.

If the résumé is the passport to the world of business, then the CV is the passport to academic and professional positions (Hodges & Connelly, 2010). Passports and CVs contain vital information about one's qualifications, and if

---

From the Trenches—Applicant Experiences and Advice

Create a version of your CV that you like (organization, visual aesthetics) early on in graduate school. I did almost nothing to my CV before applying for jobs because I took the time in my 3rd year or so to make my CV presentable. I added items and tweaked a few things over the years, which meant I didn't have to stress about the CV during the application process.

—Jennifer V., PhD in psychology

not updated, passports and CVs do expire. Along your career path, you will continue to "stamp" your CV as your qualifications, skills, and experiences expand over the course of your academic and professional life. However, before we get started on making your CV memorable, presentable, and ready for stamping, we must clarify some terminology.

Curriculum Vitae Versus Résumé Versus Dossier

Vitae translates from the Latin as "life", and the translation of *curriculum vitae* is "course of life" or "academic life." The well-kept CV is a constantly updated document that includes a comprehensive (longitudinal) but concise enumeration of your professional experiences, skills, abilities, and competencies (Kuther, 2008). The purpose of the CV is to give the potential employer an accurate snapshot of your professional skills and abilities (Crossman & Nazzaro, 1976). Simpson (2006) also described the CV as a teaching tool for you and for others, because developing and distributing it gives you and others an insight into what you have accomplished.

In contrast, the *résumé* is typically a one- to two-page summary or autobiographical sketch of one's employment history and qualifications for a job in business or industry (Crossman & Nazzaro, 1976), with the goal of focusing attention on the strongest qualifications of an applicant for a particular job or career category (Simpson, 2006). Here, brevity is paramount, as is clearly and directly providing evidence of your fulfillment of the requirements for the position. For example, when applying for government positions, your posted résumé will be electronically searched for key words whose absence will be used to filter your application out of the hands of the human resources department before even reaching the hiring committee.

An applicant's *dossier* refers to the set of documents collected by the search committee (for either an academic or professional position). The CV or résumé would certainly be one of those documents (Simpson, 2006); other documents, described in other chapters of this book, are the cover letter, the teaching statement, the research statement, publication reprints or preprints, and so on. Think of the dossier as the totality of your application package.

Make sure that you consult with your colleagues and mentors about not only the accuracy of what should be presented on your vitae but also whether an item should be included or not. If there are questions about how an item should be categorized, senior-level colleagues or mentors should be able to assist you (Simpson, 2006).

The Bones of the Curriculum Vitae

A good CV (Caplan, 1993; Kuther, 2008) would be aligned with the mission of the type of institution you are applying for (Simpson, 2006), which means that your expertise and experiences that are most closely aligned with the position you are seeking should be emphasized, either through placement (i.e., including the information toward the beginning of the document) or through providing expanded details and information. Regardless, CVs are generally organized around these major sections: (a) academic demographics; (b) professional affiliations, leadership or service positions; (c) scholarship evidence judged by peers; and (d) faculty or professional roles.

Although the order of the presentation of this information can vary, typically, a CV or résumé begins with contact information. The first item on a CV for a job candidate directly out of graduate school will start with the candidate's education listed in reverse chronological order. Frequently, the title and even a brief description of the dissertation and/or master's thesis will be included in this section (Purdue Online Writing Lab, 2011). The conventions for what information follows this are specific to your discipline; reviewing examples of CVs from those employed in your desired field will be most useful. For example, when applying for a research-oriented academic position, the next items on the CV will typically cover research interests, publications (delineating those that are refereed and not refereed), under-review and in-preparation manuscripts, conference presentations, grants and funding, research experience (in reverse chronological order), and research honors and awards. When applying for a teaching-oriented academic position, your CV should lead with your teaching interests, courses taught (including enrollment), other teaching experience (including teaching assistantships and student mentoring), and professional development experience (e.g., courses on teaching or workshops completed). Academic CVs typically end with sections listing your affiliations with professional organizations, professional and community service activities (if relevant), and contact information for your references.

Whether you are preparing an academic or professional CV, you should include all or most of the following sections and subsections:

- Contact/Personal Information
- Education and Training (Degrees)
- Employment History, Military Service (if applicable)
- Current Rank or Position
- Honors and Awards
- Grants Awarded, Grants Proposed/Pending
- Teaching Experience / Courses Taught
- Publications (Refereed, Nonrefereed)
- Conference Presentations
- Books, Book Chapters, Other Types of Publications (e.g., Technical Reports)
- Unpublished or "In preparation" Manuscripts
- Professional Service (Leadership or Editorial Positions; Memberships)
- Community Service (Membership, Leadership Positions)
- Professional Affiliations

When applying for academic positions specifically, include these sections:

- Research Experience
- Research Interests
- Statistical Experience
- Teaching Interests
- Additional Teaching Experience (e.g., mentoring or supervision of research assistants)
- Course Descriptions

For professional jobs, you should highlight categories such as the following:

- Licensures and Certifications / Board Certifications
- Clinical Experience
- Provision of Supervision (Type, Supervisee Characteristics)

Even though these skeletal outlines seem long enough, a CV can be specialized and customized even further. Hodges and Connelly (2010) generated a list of possible categories and subheadings that you might find on a CV; see Exhibit 3.1 for possible ways to communicate your education, training, and experiences. One option for organizing the CV is presented in Figure 3.1.

Make sure that your CV is available electronically (Simpson, 2006) for easy updating in Microsoft Word or to print to a PDF for an easier e-mail exchange. Many different Word add-ons can allow you to print directly from a Word file and to a PDF (the PDF actually becomes one of the printer selections in the drop-down menu).

In the detailed advice sections that follow, we examine how both the common and unique characteristics of academic and professional

---

EXHIBIT 3.1

Potential Curriculum Vitae Categories

Abstracts	Foreign Languages
Academic Background	Graduate Research Assistantships
Ancillary Materials	Graduate Teaching Assistantships
Area of Specialization	Grants and Contracts
Areas of Expertise	Honors
Awards	Journal Articles
Book Chapters	Major Area
Books	Major Committees
Career Highlights	Master's Thesis
Certification	Military Experience
Committee Chair	Minor Area
Computer Skills	Overseas Experience
Conference Presentations	Professional Memberships
Consulting	Professional Studies
Counseling Experience	Publications
Degrees	Reviewer
Dissertation	Service
Dissertation Committee Service	Supplementary Materials
Editorial Boards	Technical Reports
Education	

Note. Data from Hodges and Connelly (2010).

CVs are created. Ultimately, what you choose to include or emphasize in your CV should be related to the conventions of your discipline as well to the type of position for which you are applying (such as a clinical vs. administrative professional position or a teaching-oriented vs. research-oriented academic position). Exhibit 3.2 provides a detailed look at how departmental search committees evaluate components of the CV. The data presented there might also help you gain insight into the search process as a whole.

Curricula Vitae for Academic Positions and a Sample Curriculum Vitae

There are a variety of academic guides that provide advice and template examples of how to create an academic CV (Darley, Zanna, & Roediger, 2004; Jackson & Geckeis, 2003). However, there is not much evidence-

FIGURE 3.1

Curriculum Vitae

Name (once you graduate, write *Name, PsyD/PhD*)

Address, phone number, and e-mail address

Education

Include all doctoral, masters and bachelor degrees received; most recent degree comes first. Write out master and bachelor degrees.

Student Example (currently obtaining doctorate degree):

Doctoral Student in Clinical Psychology, APA-accredited PsyD program

Your University, Graduate School of Psychology, Anywhere, US, Anticipated Date of Graduation, Month/Year

Graduate Example (already obtained doctorate degree):

PsyD in Clinical Psychology

Your University, Graduate School of Psychology, Anywhere, US, Month/Year Dissertation Defense Date:

Dissertation Title:

Masters of Arts in Clinical Psychology

Your University, Anywhere, US, Month/Year

Bachelor of Arts in Psychology, (date is optional—Month/Year) Any University, Los Angeles, CA

Languages

If multilingual, including Sign Language

Experience (separate by category—Professional, Research, and/or Teaching)

Include—title, agency name, City/State and dates of employment (Month/Year); Awards and Honors received (can be listed as a separate section).

Example:

Pre-Intern

ABC Agency

Anywhere, US

Month/Year–Month/Year

For Research Experience only, also include

Supervisor's Name

Brief Description of Study

Add bullets describing your responsibilities

Grants and Fellowships

Use for grants received and grants written, but not funded (fine for a student/young professional).

Example:

Small Grants Division, National Institute of Mental Health, #MH36998-03, Social Skills Training for Sexual Deviants, $10,000, 1986–1987. E. Z. Dozit, Principal Investigator

Presentations and Publications (listed as two separate headings)

If submitted but not yet accepted or in progress, say so.

Start with the most recent.

Use APA style, except use single-spacing.

The bones of the curriculum vitae.

FIGURE 3.1 *(Continued)*

Examples:
Presentations
Landrum. R. E., & Murdnal, C. (2003, April).*When the spelling of a name is reversed: Does anyone notice?* Poster presented at the meeting of the Rocky Mountain Psychological Association, Reno, NV.

Publications
Smith, T., & Murdnal, C. (2004). Assigning the appropriate (high) value to reaching. *College Student Journal*, *49*, 521–529.

Professional Activities
Continuing Education, Professional Workshops, Conferences, and/or Clinical Training

Professional Organizations
If you are still a member and if it is related to job you are seeking

Professional Qualifications
Certifications and computer skills

References available upon request
List on a separate sheet of paper.

How to Write Your Job/Volunteer Responsibilities
- No "I" Statements
- Write current position in present tense and former positions in past tense
- Clear and well-organized
- Concise: summary of your background and skills
- Use bullets or paraphrases—under recent or related position list 5–6 bullets. 3–4 bullets for older jobs and jobs not related the position you are seeking
- Do not end with a period
- Write your responsibilities using the Action + Results format
  - Begin with an action verb to describe the type of work you did
  - Include a word that describes the results or intended results of your work
    - *Example: Coach parents on discipline techniques, communication, and boundary setting to foster responsibility in home, academic and social settings*
  - Sample Results Words—resulting in, to foster, in order to, to ensure
  - Use action words

Things You May Want to include in Your Psychology Related EXPERIENCE Bullets
- Type of therapy conducted (individual, family, group)
- Type of approach (e.g., CBT, Psychoanalytic, Eclectic, Behavioral)
- Type of population(s) you work(ed) with (e.g., at risk, special ed)
- Specific type of disability/presenting problems (e.g., dual diagnosis, Axis I, Anxiety, Depressed, Autistic, ADHD, developmentally delayed)
- Age of clients you work(ed) with (children, adolescents, adults)
- Type of environment you work(ed) in (e.g., school, group home, clinic)
- Experience collaborating with other professionals (e.g., teachers, therapists, physiatrist)
- Paperwork experience (if you had DMH experience, include it)
- Social work experience (assessments, intakes, and referrals)
- Testing and Assessments (included names used)
- Research Experience (testing assessment used)

The bones of the curriculum vitae.

EXHIBIT 3.2

What the Literature Says . . . About How Faculty Search Teams Evaluate Applicant Curricula Vitae

It is a bit surprising that with the cumulative effort and resources invested in the search for faculty applicants each year in the United States there is not more literature available on the topic, especially literature that is psychology-specific. Consider the magnitude of the decision-making processes in the search processes (Gmelch & Miskin, 1995);

> No other decision your department will make will be as important as the selection of a faculty colleague. Deliberate and careful selection of new colleagues has more to do with the growth and well-being of your department than any other action you may take. You are adding a family member to your department culture. Assuming that faculty exercise little mobility in their professional careers, the faculty you recruit today will be yours for life. This is a million-dollar decision—both in terms of financial resources and in terms of psychic satisfaction. You cannot afford a bad decision. (p. 19)

You can see that this would apply as easily to professional positions as it does to academic positions. Adding that new counselor or clinical psychologist or industrial and organizational psychologist to your practice could make work life more blissful or more stressful. Indeed, hiring decisions are incredibly important.

In the context of hiring an assistant professor for a department of psychology, Landrum and Clump (2004) surveyed 89 directors of departmental search committees to extract detailed information about how search decisions are made, whether that involved the preparation of materials, the inclusion or exclusion of documents, whether the dossier arrived on time, and a host of other factors. One section of the survey asked about level of agreement for 60 items, and another section asked for an importance rating for 30 items. The top 10 responses are reproduced here. The survey items were answered on a Likert-type agreement scale from 1 = *strongly disagree* to 5 = *strongly agree*.

Item	M	SD
It is important that the position applied for in the cover letter is the same as the position advertised.	4.56	0.56
Teaching experience at the undergraduate level is important for applicants.	4.43	0.77
How well a candidate matches or fits with our current teaching needs is an important consideration.	4.41	0.74
How well a candidate matches or fits with our current faculty is an important consideration.	4.36	0.80
It is important for applicants to list (somewhere in their materials) the research underway and plans for future research.	4.31	0.73
It is important for an applicant to list the courses he or she is interested in teaching.	4.11	0.76
It is a problem if the courses the applicant is interested in teaching do not match the courses mentioned in our job advertisement.	4.09	0.92

(continued)

EXHIBIT 3.2 (*Continued*)

Item	M	SD
On a curriculum vitae, conference presentations should be presented in chronological order rather than alphabetical order by author.	4.08	0.96
The absence of a letter of recommendation from the applicant's primary mentor is a cause of concern.	4.08	0.79
If our job advertisement asks for three letters of recommendation and the candidate does not include three, this is a problem.	4.06	0.68

It is good to have some insight into what practices matter to departmental search committee members. Remember that individual differences do apply, however. For instance, although respondents tended to disagree with the item "An application package that arrives extra early gives the applicant an advantage in the hiring process," there may be some members of a search committee who are highly impressed when applications arrive extra early. Perhaps those members perceive such applicants as highly organized, highly motivated, and "on the ball." Not only do some specific advice recommendations emerge from these data, but there are also value statements included, such as the relative value of teaching, research, grant activity, and so on.

Search committee respondents also rated the importance of 30 items using a scale from 1 = *not at all important* to 4 = *extremely important*. The top 10 results are as follows.

Items	M	SD
Match or fit with department	3.84	0.40
Research experience	3.61	0.61
Accuracy of application materials	3.59	0.67
Quality of publications	3.55	0.68
Teaching experience	3.43	0.75
Ensuring that three letters of recommendation arrive	3.33	0.62
Quantity of publications	3.23	0.82
Reputation of letter of recommendation writers	3.06	0.77
Quality of applicant's graduate program	2.95	0.69
Well-organized curriculum vitae	2.90	0.86

Not only are these data valuable as an insight into how departmental search committees evaluate components of the curriculum vitae but they also indicate general views about the entirety of the search process.

based literature about what makes a vitae effective; this is unfortunate because when applying for academic positions in psychology, a CV is requested by 96.1% of institutions, the highest percentage across institutions of all types and sizes (Clifton & Buskist, 2005). Brems, Lampman, and Johnson (1995) asked departmental search committees detailed questions about numerous aspects of the academic job search process and the types of information sought in a CV. It is striking that nearly 40% of applicants failed to report the specialty area of their advanced degree and that almost 30% did not include a list of referees. These types of omissions may lead to an instant disqualification in the minds of some members of the department search committee.

That applicants failed to provide complete information in key areas, such as research interests and teaching interests, is also quite surprising. Perhaps because applicants included separate teaching and research statements in their dossier, they believed this information could be left out of the CV. However, applicants for academic positions should also include brief or bulleted information about teaching and research interests on the CV for those search committee members who use the CV as the first item to be reviewed and as the litmus test to determine whether further review is warranted. Furthermore, many human resources offices require review sheets that include information typically found in the applicant's CV, and if that information is not readily available, the frustration at searching through your materials to find your current place of employment, for example, might result in a negative evaluation of your candidacy.

In addition, Brems et al. (1995) reported that there were identifiable errors present in many applications. The common errors (with percentage occurrence) included mixing of publications and presentations (20.9%); excessive personal information (38.9%); mixing of publications, work under review, and work in progress (41.2%); and violation of American Psychological Association (APA) format in citations (74.1%). Listing one's publications allows the applicant to demonstrate her or his ability to conform to APA style and format, yet 74.1% violated APA format. Over 40% of applicants mixed manuscripts in preparation, submitted manuscripts, and published manuscripts in the same section of the CV, making one's productivity appear higher at first. Finally, nearly 40% reported excessive personal information. Perhaps the best way to guard against these errors is to make sure your mentor and trusted colleagues review your CV before you submit your applications for academic positions. Given the number of applicants to the number of positions available, you should do all that you can to make you and your application materials attractive to members of the departmental search committee.

In addition to avoiding the types of errors in the CV that are common across academia, it is also important to recognize that different types of academic institutions might have different expectations for what is included or emphasized in a CV. In a survey of 89 departmental search committees, Landrum and Clump (2004) found differing opinions on what specific elements to include in the CV, depending on characteristics of the institution. In addition to asking participants to rate their agreement with 60 Likert-type statements and to rate the importance of 30 items using a 4-point importance scale (see Exhibit 3.2), these faculty members were also asked to indicate whether their department was an undergraduate-only department or a department with both undergraduate and graduate programs. The two types of departments differed significantly, as one would expect, on responses to the item "An applicant's curriculum vitae should include undergraduate courses taught," with undergraduate-only department participants agreeing with this item significantly more than combined undergraduate and graduate program participants. The overall conclusions that can be drawn from all the studies in this area are that a "one-size-fits-all" approach is not likely to be successful and attention to detail is necessary in order to satisfy different CV requirements.

Figure 3.2 presents the academic CV of Dr. Jennifer Weaver, a relatively recent academic hire at Boise State University. Several points about this CV are worthy of note. First, notice that complete dates are provided for each item; this is informative and shows attention to detail. Second, the brief descriptions of the applicant's professional positions are excellent; note that these do not need to be presented as complete sentences. In addition, note the variety of action verbs Jennifer used in her "Professional Positions" and "Teaching Experience" sections. Her use of action verbs gives a clear picture of her experience and competencies. (For a nearly exhaustive list of action verbs you might use to describe your strengths and potential contributions, visit http://www.bc.edu/offices/careers/skills/resumes/verbs.html.) Note also that the publications and presentations are listed in perfect APA Style. Moreover, Jennifer has also included a "Manuscripts in Preparation" section, which shows that she has a "pipeline"; that is, she has an active program of research underway. If, as in this CV, you choose to include "Courses Prepared to Teach," make sure you match the courses you list to those available at the university you are applying to. This will mean customizing your CV according to the requirement of the school to which you are applying. Finally, keep track

---

From the Trenches—Applicant Experiences and Advice

I applied for faculty positions that were more teaching oriented as well as some postdocs. For postdocs, I ordered my CV in such a way that my research experience came before teaching experience. I did the opposite for the teaching oriented positions.

—Jordon T., PhD in psychology, adjunct instructor at a large research university in the Northeast

FIGURE 3.2

Jennifer Miner Weaver
Curriculum Vitae

Family Research Center
University of North Carolina, Greensboro
1123 Park Ave
PO Box 555
Town, NC 99999
jmweaver@email.com
Ph: (555) 317-5051

EDUCATION

University of California, Irvine

PhD, Psychology and Social Behavior (Developmental Psychology; Minor in Statistics and Research Methods) 2009

Dissertation: *Setting the tone: Understanding how the family context transmits risk for children of parents with depressive symptoms and high levels of anger.*

Dissertation Committee: Dr. K. Alison Clarke-Stewart (chair), Dr. Wendy Goldberg, Dr. Deborah Vandell, and Dr. Ross Parke

MA in Social Ecology 2005

Master's Thesis: *Relations between parenting, temperament, and children's externalizing trajectories from 24 months to 3rd Grade.*

University of Oregon, Clark Honors College
BA in Psychology 2003
Summa cum Laude, Phi Beta Kappa, Departmental Honors
Honors Thesis: *Parental attitudes toward pretend play and imaginary companions in preschoolers.*

FELLOWSHIPS AND HONORS

Social Ecology Dean's Dissertation Writing Fellowship, Univ of California, Irvine	2009
Social Ecology Dean's Dissertation Data Analysis Fellowship, Univ of California, Irvine	2008
NIMH Training Grant recipient, University of California, Irvine	2004–2006
Social Ecology Dean's Fellowship, University of California, Irvine	2003
Presidential Scholar, University of Oregon	1999–2003
Psi Chi, National Honor Society for Psychology	2003

RESEARCH INTERESTS

- Parenting and the family's role in children's social development, including externalizing, and internalizing symptoms
- How risks in children's environments may alter their developmental trajectories over time, such as parental mental health problems, divorce, or inadequate parenting
- Adoptive parent–child relationships

Example of an academic curriculum vitae. Copyright 2009 by Jennifer Miner Weaver. Printed with permission.

FIGURE 3.2 (*Continued*)

Weaver CV 2

PROFESSIONAL POSITIONS

Postdoctoral Research Associate, University of North Carolina, Greensboro
Mentor: Dr. Marion O'Brien
Participating in an on-going longitudinal study looking at the cognitive, emotional, and physiological contributors to early school success. Duties include manuscript preparation, assisting in grant writing activities, bi-weekly meetings with study PIs, and mentoring graduate students.

Fall 2009–present

Data Collection Trainer for the National Children's Study, UC, Irvine
Led and conducted week-long, in-depth training sessions with field workers on data collection procedures for the enumeration and recruitment phase of this national study.

March–June 2009

National Children's Study Lister, UC, Irvine
Mapped study segments in Orange County, CA, in preparation for participant recruitment. Assisted Dr. Haiou Yang in overseeing the work of eight other research assistants.

Aug–Sept 2008

Research Assistant, NICHD Study of Early Child Care and Youth Development, UC, Irvine
Participated in Phase IV of data collection for this national study. Involved in piloting instruments, writing protocol manuals, running laboratory visits with adolescents, and meeting weekly with study PIs (Dr. Alison Clarke-Stewart and Dr. Elizabeth Cauffman).

July 2005–Dec 2006

Research Assistant, Mother–Infant Interaction Project, UC, Irvine
Developed protocol for mother-infant interaction, coded maternal sensitivity, trained undergraduate assistants in coding, and oversaw their reliability.

2003–2005

Research Assistant, NICHD Study of Early Child Care and Youth Development, UC, Irvine
Coded videotaped interactions of study child with his/her best friend.

June–Aug 2003

Research Assistant, Oregon Research Institute, Eugene, OR
Worked on the Understanding Personality project overseen by Dr. Lewis Goldberg and Dr. Gerard Saucier. Participated in data collection, cleaned and entered data, and attended weekly research meetings.

2002–2003

Research Assistant, University of Oregon
Imagination Lab, supervised by Dr. Marjorie Taylor. Learned assessment protocol for preschoolers, trained new RA's, and attended weekly research seminar.

2002–2003

Research Assistant, University of Oregon
Gene-Environment Process lab, supervised by Dr. Kirby Deater-Deckard. Coded parent–child interactions, trained new RA's, cleaned and entereed data, and attended lab meetings.

2001–2002

Research Assistant, University of Oregon
Memory Lab, supervised by Dr. Michael Anderson. Administered laboratory experiments; trained new assistants; coded, entered, and analyzed data for reports; recruited participants; and assisted in the design of new experiments.

2000–2001

Example of an academic curriculum vitae. Copyright 2009 by Jennifer Miner Weaver. Printed with permission.

FIGURE 3.2 (Continued)

Weaver CV   3

Data Collector, University of Oregon   1999–2000
School Psychology research project. Visited area Head Start programs and
elementary schools; administered assessment protocols, including cognitive
and literacy tests; and made observational assessments of children in school settings.

PUBLICATIONS

O'Brien. M., Weaver, J. M., Nelson, J., Calkins, S. D., Leerkes, E. M., & Marcovitch, S. (in press). Longitudinal
associations between children's understanding of emotions and theory of mind. *Cognition & Emotion.*

Clarke-Stewart, K. A., & Miner, J. L. (2008) Effects of child and day care. In M. Haith & J. B. Benson (Eds.),
Encyclopedia of infant and early childhood development (pp. 268–278). San Diego, CA: Academic Press.

Miner, J. L. (2008). Adolescents in Orange County, CA: Family influences on the development of task
motivation in adolescents. In J. B. Miner, *Organizational behavior 5: From unconscious motivation to
role-motivated leadership* (pp. 304–320). Armonk, NY: M. E. Sharpe.

Miner, J. L. (2008). Factor analysis of the Miner Sentence Completion Scales. In J. B. Miner, *Organizational
behavior 5: From unconscious motivation to role-motivated leadership* (pp. 421–435). Armonk, NY: M
E. Sharpe.

Miner, J. L., & Clarke-Stewart, K. A. (2008). Trajectories of externalizing behavior from age 2 to age 8:
Relations with gender, temperament, parenting, and rater. *Developmental Psychology, 44,* 771–786.

Allhusen, V. D, Clarke-Stewart, K. A., & Miner, J. L. (2006). Child care in the United States: Characteristics and
consequences. In E. Melhuish & K. Petrogiannis (Eds.), *Early childhood care & education:
International perspectives* (pp. 7–26). London, England: Routledge.

Manuscripts in Preparation

Weaver, J. M., Schofield, T., & Clarke-Stewart, K. A. (invited to revise and resubmit). A longitudinal
examination of divorce effects on children's internalizing and externalizing behavior problems.

Calkins, S. D., Weaver, J. M., Leerkes, E., Marcovitch, S., & O'Brien, M. (in preparation). Cardiac responses to
cognitive and emotional challenge in preschoolers.

Weaver, J. M., & Clarke-Stewart, K. A. (in preparation). How parental depression leads to psychological
problems in adolescence.

PROFESSIONAL PRESENTATIONS

Weaver, J. M. (2010, April). Setting the tone: *Longitudinal associations between parental anger and
depressive symptoms and adolescent adjustment.* Invited talk presented at the University of North
Carolina, Greensboro Department of Human Development and Family Studies Colloquium Series.

Weaver, J. M., & Schofield, T. (2009, April). *Longitudinal effects of divorce: The role of parenting as a
moderator.* Presented at the biennial meeting of the Society for Research and Child Development,
Denver, CO.

Weaver, J. M. (2009, April). *The depressed family: Parental depressive symptoms, the family environment,
and adolescent outcomes.* Presented at the biennial meeting of the Society for Research and Child
Development, Denver, CO.

Miner, J. L. (2007, March). *Emerging entrepreneurs? Relations between adolescent task motivation, gender and
parenting.* Poster presented at the Biennial meeting of the Society for Research and Child
Development, Boston, MA.

Example of an academic curriculum vitae. Copyright 2009 by Jennifer Miner
Weaver. Printed with permission.

FIGURE 3.2 (*Continued*)

Miner, J. L. (2007, March). *Externalizing trajectories from age 2 to age 8: Relations with gender, temperament, parenting, and rater.* Poster presented at the biennial meeting of the Society for Research and Child Development, Boston, MA.

Lucas-Thompson, R., Miner, J. L., Goldberg, W. A., Davis, E., & Sandman, C. A. (2006, July). *Mothers and infants at play: Links between maternal sensitivity and infant behavior.* Poster presented at the annual Conference for the World Association for Infant Mental Health, Paris, France.

Miner, J. L. (2006, May). *Predicting children's externalizing trajectories from early parental attitudes and behaviors.* Poster presented at the annual convention of the Association for Psychological Science, New York, New York.

TEACHING EXPERIENCE

Lecturer, California State University, Dominguez Hills   Fall 2008
"Stress, Risk and Resilience"
Developed syllabus, designed course lectures and activities, wrote exams, advised students, and graded all course material. Course was an upper division class required for the Child Development major. Enrollment: 13 students. Average student rating of teaching: 6.75/7.

Instructor of Record, University of California, Irvine   Winter 2008
"Introduction to Human Behavior" (w/ discussion sections)
Developed syllabus, wrote course lectures and exams, designed discussion section activities, met with students, oversaw four teaching assistants, and administered all grades. Course enrollment: 400 students. Average student rating of teaching: 5.4/7.

Instructor of Record, University of California, Irvine   Summer 2007
"Introduction to Human Behavior"
Developed syllabus, wrote course lectures and exams, met with students, oversaw teaching assistant, and administered all grades. Course enrollment: 80 students. Average student rating of teaching: 6.04/7.

Teaching Assistant, University of California, Irvine   Spring 2008
"Applied Statistics in Psychology"
Assisted Dr. JoAnn Prause with administering this honors level course. Taught a weekly lab section focused on using SPSS to compute ANOVA, regression, t-tests, and other statistical tests.

Teaching Assistant, University of California, Irvine   Fall 2007 &
"Sports Psychology"   2008
Assisted Dr. Stehpanie McEwan with administering all grades for class. Held weekly office hours and gave a lecture on character development in sports.

Teaching Assistant, University of California, Irvine   Winter 2007
"Adolescent Development"
Assisted Dr. Terry Webster with administering course for 100+ students, maintained course website, advised students on their research papers for the course, and held review sessions before exams as well as weekly office hours.

Courses Prepared to Teach
I am prepared to teach courses related to child and adolescent development, introductory psychology, statistics and research methods, lifespan development, developmental psychopathology, parenting, the role of the family in child development, and risk and resilience in childhood.

Example of an academic curriculum vitae. Copyright 2009 by Jennifer Miner Weaver. Printed with permission.

FIGURE 3.2 *(Continued)*

PROFESSIONAL ACTIVITIES

Attendee, Course Design Workshop: University of California, Irvine	May 2007
Attendee, APA Advanced Training Institute: NICHD Study of Early Child Care and Youth Development	June 2005
Attendee, Workshop on SAS statistical program: University of California, Irvine	Dec 2004
Ad hoc reviewer for *Sex Roles*, *Journal of Abnormal Child Psychology*, and *Learning and Individual Differences*	

PROFESSIONAL MEMBERSHIPS

American Psychological Association (Division 7 member)
Society for Research in Child Development
Association for Psychological Science (APS)

PROFESSIONAL REFERENCES

Dr. K. Alison Clarke-Stewart
University of California, Irvine
Psychology and Social Behavior
33 A Building
Irvine, CA 92697
Phone: (555) 331-2001
acstewar@email.com

Dr. Wendy Goldberg
University of California, Irvine
Psychology and Social Behavior
33 A Building
Irvine, CA 92697
Phone: (555) 331-2002
wagoldbe@email.com

Dr. Marion O'Brien
University of North Carolina at Greensboro
123 Stone
P.O. Box 5555
Greensboro, NC 27402
Phone: (555) 052-1111
m_obrien@email.com

Example of an academic curriculum vitae. Copyright 2009 by Jennifer Miner Weaver. Printed with permission.

of your memberships in professional organizations. These should be listed in the CV along with any leadership positions assumed in these organizations.

Curricula Vitae for Professional Positions and a Sample Curriculum Vitae

For the professional position applicant, the details of the CV may vary slightly from the standard template and the academic position approach, although the goal of a CV in any scenario is to inform and persuade the reader to inquire further about the applicant (Williams-Nickelson & Prinstein, 2007). In your CV, you will highlight experiences, such as workshops or presentations you have delivered, relevant to your specialty area and your training (Hodges & Connelly, 2010). "Practitioners should emphasize the material concerning psychological practice by, for example, making the sections related to practice (e.g., Licensure, Clinical Experience) more prominent and excluding sections that are irrelevant or for which they have not experience" (Kuther, 2008, p. 218). Thus, for an applicant for a professional position, the CV might include experience as an internship training director or faculty member (Williams-Nickelson & Prinstein, 2007), predoctoral and postdoctoral appointments, and so on.

You will find conflicting advice about what to include on a CV for professional positions. For example, Hitchings and Ornellas (1999) encouraged applicants for professional positions to include a small section on the CV for leisure interests (as do Hodges & Connelly, 2010), whereas others (e.g., Williams-Nickelson & Prinstein, 2007) specifically advised against that practice. How do you resolve the conflict? First, make sure you do what is comfortable for you. Second, if you are unsure, consult your mentor(s) and trusted colleagues for their opinions about this type of information—in fact, you should ask many individuals to review drafts of your CV throughout the process. It is important to remember that composing the CV is not a one-size-fits-all process, even though academic and professional psychology are such specialty areas.

Another important consideration to keep in mind when applying for professional positions is that it is common for corporate, government, or "nonclinical" professional organizations to request a résumé instead of a CV from job applicants. This means that the employer is looking for a brief (under two pages) summary of your experiences and skills that are directly pertinent to the position you are applying for, rather than an all-encompassing lengthy CV. To convert your CV into a résumé, include only relevant skills and experiences and leave out publications and presentations except for the select few that may be directly relevant to the position for which you are applying, remove your references, and use consistent formatting (Thompson & Wein, 2004).

When creating your CV for applied, professional positions, you may have to make substantial revisions to your preexisting CV, which may be a trainee CV in which you provided high amounts of detail about each experience during your supervision (Chin, 2009). However, even in your newly edited CV for professional position applications, be sure to list licenses and permits with certificate number, for example, Nationally Certified Counselor (NCC #49346) (Hodges & Connelly, 2010, p. 37).

A sample CV for a person seeking a professional position in psychology presented in Figure 3.3.

FIGURE 3.3

Sarah M. Heavin, PhD
LICENSED CLINICAL PSYCHOLOGIST

CURRICULUM VITAE

EDUCATION

Senior Fellow	**University of Washington** (2009-2010) Postdoctoral Fellowship in Juvenile Forensic Psychology and Adolescent Inpatient Treatment
Ph.D.	**University of Utah** (2009) Clinical Psychology, Child and Family Specialization Dissertation Title: Evaluating the Efficacy of a Brief Coparenting Intervention for Adolescents: Improving Parenting Attitudes, Stress and Behavior. (Chair, Dr. Paul Florsheim, Ph.D.)
Clinical Internship	**Western State Hospital** (2008-2009) APA Approved Rotations: Program for Forensic Evaluations in Community and Corrections, Child Study and Treatment Center, Special Commitment Center
M.S.	**University of Utah** (2006) Master of Science in Psychology Thesis title: Manipulation of Craving in Substance Abusing Adolescents (Chair, Dr. Paul Florsheim, Ph.D.)
B.S.	**Boise State University** (2002) Bachelor of Science in Psychology

PUBLICATIONS

Florsheim, P., McArthur, L., Hudak, C., Heavin, S., & Burrow-Sanchez, J. (2011) The Young Parenthood Program: A co-parenting counseling program for pregnant adolescents and young expectant fathers. *Journal of Couple and Relationship Therapy, 10*(2), 117–134.

Lexcen, F., Heavin, S., & Redick, C. (2010). A clinical application of the Juvenile Adjudicative Competence Interview (JACI). *Open Access Journal of Forensic Psychology*, 2, 287–305.

Lexcen, F., & Heavin, S., (2010). Evaluating for competence to proceed in juvenile court: Findings with a semi-structured interview. *Open Access Journal of Forensic Psychology*, 2, 359–376.

Florsheim, P., Heavin, S., Tiffany, S., Colvin, P., & Hiraoka, R. (2007). An experimental test of craving management techniques for adolescents in substance-abuse treatment. *Journal of Youth and Adolescence, 37,* 1205–1215. doi: 10.1007/s10964-007-9232-0

Florsheim, P., Shiozaki, T., Hiraoka, G., Tiffany, S., Heavin, S., Teske, N., & Clegg, C. (2007). Craving among polysubstance abusing adolescents. *Journal of Child and Adolescent Substance Abuse, 17*(2), 101–124.

Turrisi, R., Hillhouse, J., Heavin, S., Robinson, J., Adams, M., & Berry, J. (2004). Examination of the short-term efficacy of a parent-based intervention to prevent skin cancer. *Journal of Behavioral Medicine, 27*(4), 393–412.

123 Avenue Suite 210 Town, Virginia 23000	MOBILE 555.512.3111 OFFICE 555.512.3120 FAX 555.520.3012	sarah@email.com www.sarahdoctor.com

Example of a professional curriculum vitae. Copyright 2011 by Sarah M. Heavin. Printed with permission.

FIGURE 3.3 (*Continued*)

HONORS AND AWARDS

2006–2008	All Department Commendation, overall excellence in teaching, clinical work, and research productivity. Two time award winner, University of Utah
2007	Clinical Commendation, outstanding clinical service, University of Utah
2006	Kevin Hawley Award Winner, contributing to departmental atmosphere through academic excellence, charitable sharing of time and improving student morale, University of Utah
2004–2007	Graduate Research Travel Award, conference travel funds based on research quality and significance. Three time award winner, University of Utah
2003	Teaching Commendation, exceptional performance in the instruction of undergraduate coursework, University of Utah
2002	President's Award for Distinguished Service, given to three students recognized as role models and mentors to other student leaders and for advancing student life, Boise State University

CONFERENCE PRESENTATIONS

Florsheim, P., Hudak, C., Heavin, S., Burrow-Sanchez, J., McArthur, L., Lemke, M., . . . Paredes, R. (2010). Including young fathers in preventing repeat pregnancies among adolescent mothers: A couples program for promoting birth control. In *A public health perspective on adolescent romance and sexual behavior*. Symposium conducted at the meeting of the Society for Research on Adolescence Conference, Philadelphia, PA.

Heavin, S., Lexcen, F., & Zimmerman, E. (2010). Demographic and clinical influences on juvenile competence to stand trial. In T. Grisso (moderator). *Improving juvenile competence to stand trial evaluations: Clinical approaches, empirical results, and multi-disciplinary concerns.* Symposium conducted at the meeting of the American Psycho-Legal Society, Vancouver, British Columbia.

Olivares, I., Saenz, J., McArthur, M., Heavin, S., Paredes, R., Sanchez, . . . Florsheim, P. (2008). *An intervention for pregnant teens and their partners: Do differences in relationship security predict treatment response?* Society for Research on Adolescence Conference, Chicago, IL.

Rodriguez, M., Heavin, S., Galliher, R., & Torres, Y. (2008). *Cultural considerations in providing intervention for adolescents.* Invited oral presentation presented at the meeting of the Rocky Mountain Psychological Association, Boise, ID.

Torres, Y., Lauritzen, D., Heavin, S., & Florsheim, P. (2008). *Family relationships and risk for substance abuse: Differences between Latino and European-American young expectant fathers.* Presented at the meeting of the Rocky Mountain Psychological Association, Boise, ID.

Wrona, M., Henderson, J., Heavin, S., & Florsheim, P. (2008). *Testing a relationship focused intervention for pregnant adolescents and their partners.* Presented at the meeting of the Rocky Mountain Psychological Association, Boise, ID.

Florsheim, P., Heavin, S., & Tiffany, S. (2006). *Refining intervention science: Using experimental methods to test the mechanisms of treatment with clinical samples of adolescents.* Invited talk in honor of Daniel Offer at University of Illinois at Chicago, Institute for Juvenile Research.

Heavin, S., Colvin, P., Florsheim, P., & Tiffany, S. (2006). *Individual differences in craving experience among adolescents with substance use disorders.* Presented at the Kansas Conference in Clinical Child and Adolescent Psychology, Lawrence, KS.

Example of a professional curriculum vitae. Copyright 2011 by Sarah M. Heavin. Printed with permission.

FIGURE 3.3 (*Continued*)

Heavin, S., Colvin, P., Florsheim, P., & Tiffany, S. (2006). *Manipulating craving among adolescents with substance use disorders.* Presented at the meeting of the Rocky Mountain Psychological Association, Park City, UT.

Heavin, S., Florsheim, P., Hiraoka, R., Tiffany, S., & Teske, N. (2005). *Manipulating craving among adolescents with substance use disorders.* Presented at the meeting of the Society for Research on Alcoholism, Santa Barbara, CA

Heavin, S., Florsheim, P., Hiraoka, R., Tiffany, S., & Shiozaki, T. (2005). *Understanding and controlling craving among adolescents with substance use disorders.* Presented at the meeting of the Society for Research in Child Development, Atlanta, GA.

Hiraoka, R., Heavin, S., Randall-Stitt, C., Hall, S., Florsheim, P., & Tiffany, S. (2004). *Do adolescent substance abusers have distinct craving experiences for different drugs?* Presented at the meeting of the Rocky Mountain Psychological Association, Reno, NV.

Shiozaki, T., Florsheim, P., Tiffany, S., Heavin, S., Minen, S., & Clegg, C. (2004). *Adolescent substance abuse: Can personality predict craving?* Presented at the meeting of the Rocky Mountain Psychological Association, Reno, NV.

Heavin, S., Adams, M., Berry, J., Scremin, N., Turrisi, R., Hillhouse, J., . . . Glass, M. (2002). *Examination of the short-term efficacy of a parent-based intervention to prevent skin cancer.* Presented at the meeting of the Rocky Mountain Psychological Association, Park City, UT.

Hillhouse, J., Glass, M., Turrisi, R., Hamilton, J., & Heavin, S. (2002). *An appearance-focused intervention to reduce indoor tanning-induced UV exposure in high school students.* Presented at the meeting of the Rocky Mountain Psychological Association, Park City, UT.

Turrisi, R., Taki, R., Heavin, S., Finn, L., & Wood, E. (2001). *Examination of a parent-based intervention to reduce college student drinking tendencies.* Paper presented at the meeting of the Research Society on Alcoholism, Montreal, Quebec, Canada.

Turrisi, R., Heavin, S., Wiersmna, K., & Hughes, K. (2000). *High school behaviors as moderators in the college binge drinking-consequence relationship: The role of mother-teen communication in reducing college drinking consequences.* Paper presented at the meeting of the Research Society on Alcoholism, Denver, CO.

TEACHING EXPERIENCE

Fall 2011	Introduction to Psychology, University of Puget Sound
	Adolescent to Adult Development, University of Puget Sound
	Developmental Psychopathology, University of Puget Sound
Spring 2011	Infant and Child Development, University of Puget Sound
Fall 2010	Developmental Psychopathology, University of Puget Sound
Fall 2009	Introduction to Psychology, Distance Education, University of Utah
Summer 2009	Introduction to Psychology, Distance Education, University of Utah
Spring 2009	Introduction to Psychology, Distance Education, University of Utah
Fall 2008	Introduction to Psychology, Distance Education, University of Utah
Summer 2008	Introduction to Psychology, Distance Education, University of Utah
Summer 2006	Infancy and Child Development, University of Utah
Spring 2006	Graduate Clinical Assessment, Teaching Assistant, University of Utah
Fall 2005	Graduate Clinical Assessment, Teaching Assistant, University of Utah
Summer 2005	Abnormal Child Psychology, Graduate Instructor, University of Utah
Spring 2005	Abnormal Child Psychology, Graduate Instructor, University of Utah
Fall 2004	Abnormal Child Psychology, Graduate Instructor, University of Utah
Summer 2004	Abnormal Child Psychology, Graduate Instructor, University of Utah
Spring 2004	Research Methods, Teaching Assistant, University of Utah
Fall 2003	Abnormal Child Psychology, Teaching Assistant, University of Utah

Example of a professional curriculum vitae. Copyright 2011 by Sarah M. Heavin. Printed with permission.

FIGURE 3.3 (*Continued*)

Spring 2002	Advanced Statistical Methods, Teaching Assistant, Boise State University
Spring 2001	Child Psychopathology, Teaching Assistant, Boise State University
Fall 2001	Statistical Methods, Teaching Assistant and Paid Tutor, Boise State University

CLINICAL EXPERIENCE

Spring 2009 – *Child Study and Treatment Center* - Group and individual therapy for
Spring 2011 children and adolescents within an inpatient psychiatric hospital using Dialectical Behavior Therapy, Developmental Therapy, and Trauma-Focused Cognitive-Behavior Therapy (TF-CBT) models. Family therapy using Parent–Child Interaction Therapy (PCIT). Forensic evaluations for juvenile courts throughout Washington focused on diagnosis, competency to stand trial, mental status at time of offense, and risk for future dangerousness. Treatment for competence restoration. Training of other professionals regarding family therapy models.

Summer 2009 *Special Commitment Center* - Group and individual therapy with adults who have been civilly committed following classification as Sexually Violent Predators. Utilized a sex-offender specific therapy program focused on relapse prevention strategies.

Fall 2008 *Western State Hospital* - Comprehensive pretrial forensic mental health evaluations to the State and Limited Jurisdiction Courts in Western Washington. Evaluations focused on diagnosis, competency to stand trial, treatment recommendations for those found not competent to stand trial, criminal responsibility, danger to others, likelihood of committing offenses, and need for an involuntary treatment evaluations.

2005 – 2008 *Center for Safe and Healthy Families* - Group psychotherapy with children having sexual behavior problems and their parents. Individual psychotherapy using TF-CBT and PCIT in a University of Utah Hospital based clinic. Weekly group and individual supervision.

2006 – 2008 *Interpersonal Reconstructive Therapy Clinic* - Individual inpatient and outpatient psychotherapy with severely personality disordered adults at the University of Utah Neuropsychiatric Clinic Weekly group supervision, individual supervision, and case consultation.

2004 – 2008 *Adolescent Development and Outreach Program* - Community-based individual psychotherapy and assessment for underserved adolescents. Biweekly group and individual supervision.

2006 – 2007 *Child Therapy Practicum* - Community based individual and family therapy with children aged 11–15 utilizing the Adolescent Transitions Program. Weekly group supervision and individual supervision of undergraduate parenting consultants.

2004 – 2006 *Open Door Clinic* - Group psychotherapy with homeless adolescents in an outpatient community medical clinic. Weekly group supervision.

2004 – 2006 *Primary Children's Hospital* - Comprehensive neuropsychological assessment with medically fragile children and adolescents. Periodic individual supervision.

2004 – 2006 *Assessment Practicum* - Personality and cognitive assessment of children; adolescents; and adults at the University Counseling Center, Salt Lake School District, and Primary Children's Medical Center. Weekly group and individual supervision.

SPECIALIZED CLINICAL TRANING

Fall 2008	Criminal Forensic Foundations Seminar
Fall 2005	Functional Family Therapy Seminar
Summer 2007	Parent–Child Interaction Therapy Seminar
2006 – 2007	Motivational Interviewing Seminar
Summer 2005	Rorschach Administration and Coding Seminar
2005 – 2007	Structural Analysis of Social Behavior (SASB) Seminar

Example of a professional curriculum vitae. Copyright 2011 by Sarah M. Heavin. Printed with permission.

The Bottom Line: Top Recommendations for New Doctorates

As with any endeavor related to science, whether your training has prepared you for an academic or a professional position, you must be fair in reporting your data; this is the high ethical standard to which all psychology doctorates are held. How does this apply in the creation of your CV? For example, if there are gaps in your record, such as during graduate school or employment, these gaps should appear in your CV. For example, if you took some time off ("stepped out," not dropped out) to start a family, your CV will have a gap in time, which careful reading will reveal. Do not fill the gap with vague descriptions such as "paternal case study" or "domestic engineer"; just leave the gap as it is. If asked about it in a job interview, be truthful. If you took time off during your doctoral studies to start a family and a search committee holds that gap in your training against you, perhaps it is not the type of place at which you want to work.

Another common occurrence on the CVs of new doctorates is the combining of related work areas into one category to make that category appear lengthier. If you are applying for an academic position and you list only one publication but two other manuscripts submitted for publication and three other manuscripts that you are working on in the "Publications" section of your CV, do not list six publications. Be fair with the data: Use separate headings for "Publications," "Submitted Manuscripts," and "Work in Progress." Similarly, do not mix your publications and conference presentations under one heading to hide that you do not have as many publications as you would like to. A benefit of separating your publications, submissions, and works in progress is that you demonstrate to search committees that you have a pipeline; that is, you are continually working on research projects that are at various stages of the publication process.

Research Statements, Teaching Statements, and Teaching Portfolios

4

A quick browse of job advertisements posted on websites such as the *Chronicle of Higher Education* (http://chronicle.com/section/Jobs/61) will provide you with a good idea of what types of materials are most often requested in applications for academic and professional positions (Chapter 2, this volume, also presents some sample job advertisements). The standard materials requested for professional positions, such as those with nonprofit or government agencies, educational organizations, or consultancy groups, are a cover letter or letter of interest, a résumé or curriculum vitae (CV), and perhaps a list of references. The majority of applications for academic positions require a research statement, teaching statement, and/or teaching portfolio (Clifton & Buskist, 2005), although these often go by different names (e.g., statement of research interests, teaching philosophy, evidence of teaching excellence). What committees are looking for in these documents is supplemental information about your research and teaching abilities beyond that already provided in your cover letter and your CV.

In this chapter, we review the purpose, components, and typical structure of each of these elements of your job application. Thus, the remainder of this chapter is most applicable to individuals preparing to apply for academic positions. Nonetheless, the suggestions we provide for these documents can have benefits that extend beyond simply procuring gainful employment; they can also provide you with the opportunity to engage in thoughtful reflection about your research agenda and approach your teaching more purposefully. In addition, at the end of the chapter there is a brief section on supplemental documents occasionally requested for applications to professional positions.

Keep in mind that research statements, teaching statements, and teaching portfolios are not meant to replace or simply replicate your CV; they serve a unique, more detailed purpose. Furthermore, they often are not rated as highly as the CV and cover letter in importance, particularly during the first round of decision making. Whether they are requested with your original application or once you have been selected for an interview, it is possible that they may not be closely read until the committee is ready to make a second or final cut (J. Austin, 2002). At this point, they would become even more central in the job selection process, so producing top-quality materials is critical.

Departmental fit, a good teaching record, and a good record of research experience are often in the top three criteria that search committees and department chairs cite for evaluating candidates (Burns & Kinkade, 2008; Landrum & Clump, 2004). In fact, Sheehan, McDevitt, and Ross (1998) examined the criteria that academic departments used to evaluate job applicants and found that after the letter of recommendation, the next most important criteria were (a) fit between applicant's research and departmental needs, (b) experience in teaching courses related to the position description, (c) general teaching experience, and (d) quality of course evaluations. Preparing a portfolio that includes both teaching and research interests provides you with an important opportunity to demonstrate your suitability for the position for which you are applying. Preparation of these documents also provides potential future employers with samples of your writing abilities and organizational skills.

It is important to recognize that there are extensive variations of these documents. In reality, there is not a gold standard or one-size-fits-all formula for preparing these materials. This is most obvious in the job advertisements themselves. The terms used for these types of documents vary from place to place, and it is common for a variety of constellations of supplemental documents to be requested. For example, a research statement may be requested without a teaching statement (or vice versa). Some institutions may ask for joint teaching and research statements, whereas others may ask only for a teaching portfolio or evaluations, without any mention of a statement or philosophy.

Despite the frustration job seekers might feel when dealing with these variations, attending to these details can actually be useful. For example, the supplemental materials that are requested your application can give you some insight into what the department most values. If a teaching statement is required, but not a research statement, this obviously tells you that the department is interested in more detailed information about your teaching and is not as interested in information about your program of research. Thus, you can modify your cover letter and CV accordingly and take these considerations into account in future communications with the institution.

Although the most commonly requested application materials for assistant professor positions include a cover letter, CV, references, reprints, research statement, and teaching statement (Clifton & Buskist, 2005), academic institutions have been known to request other items as well. The following is a list of items that are rarely requested but that you should be prepared to produce if necessary:

- statement of minimum laboratory needs or start-up needs,
- graduate transcripts,
- statement of your vision for psychology,
- statement of leadership efforts and/or contributions to diversity,
- response to the mission statement of the institution, and
- completed standard application form.

In general, you should use some judgment in amending these documents to meet the specific requests of each school or organization. Often, submitting research and teaching statements when they are not specifically requested is considered acceptable, whereas a teaching portfolio and reprints should only be submitted when specifically requested. Submitting documents because you have them (even though they are not requested) may not always be helpful. Furthermore, if a combined document is requested and you send separate ones, you run the risk

---

From the Trenches—Employer Experiences and Advice

Attachments should be those that were requested. Omitting teaching evaluations, for example, is very frustrating. Incomplete applications do not let you evaluate applicants appropriately and having to contact them for additional materials takes time we frequently don't have. On a related note, when they include materials that were *not* requested, it is equally frustrating (e.g., a packet of research papers when you are at a teaching college). Providing materials like a research statement that are *not* requested make it clear the person doesn't read instructions or simply doesn't care. We usually dump these people's materials no matter how good they look in the cover letter or CV.

—Kelly J., PhD in social psychology, assistant professor at a private college in the Northeast

of being seen as incapable of following directions and likely as less interested in the position (because you did not tailor your application appropriately). You can avoid submitting unsolicited materials while still providing detailed information about your program of research and teaching philosophy by extending your discussion of these topics in your cover letter; however, your statements should be well integrated and highly abbreviated. Overall, be careful about submitting an application that does not precisely follow the instructions in the job advertisement, and recognize that unsolicited supplemental materials may help or hinder your application. When in doubt, try to contact someone from the search committee for more details about the requested documents. This can also give you the added benefit of making a personal contact with the department of interest.

Research Statements

A common component of the academic job application is a document that describes your research area, program of research, and future research plans. Job postings may request this document using a number of different names, including a "description of your research," a "statement of planned research," a "statement of research plans," an "outline of your research program," a "statement of research interests," or a "research summary." Regardless of the term used, most committees will be looking for the same type of document. Of course, if specific directions are given in the advertisement that run counter to the typical research statement, you should cater to those requests.

PURPOSE AND COMMON COMPONENTS

When you are applying for an academic or professional research position, it is expected that you have thought about your research beyond completing your dissertation. Therefore, the research statement should convey to the committee that you have an active, ongoing, and coherent program of research (or that you are actively planning a program of research if you have not yet established one). To determine whether you will be able to pursue that line of research successfully at their institution, it is also likely that the committee will be reviewing this document and assessing your compatibility with the department or school, your areas of specialty, your abilities as an independent researcher, and your potential to get grants (Career Services, University of Pennsylvania, n.d.). Thus, the research statement becomes an opportunity to provide the search committee with a "compelling, reassuring, believable image of what their life will be like when you are working down the hall" (J. Austin, 2002, para. 10).

Although being hired is likely your main purpose for writing the research statement, it also serves another important function. Because a research statement is essentially a plan for your career in research (in the short run, at least) that coherently demonstrates your intellectual vision and aspirations, writing this document is in itself an act of professional development. Through writing your research statement, you can formally ask yourself whether you are pursuing a worthy line of research that you would be willing to work on for years to come. Does this line of research excite you? Do you have a vision for where your research is heading? Are you driven to pursue this vision? If you find yourself toward the end of your doctoral education without answers to these questions, and you need to develop a research statement for a job application, it would be a good time to speak with your advisor or other mentors about your program of research, to assess whether you are well positioned to enter the job market or whether you might need to take more time to establish yourself as a researcher. In addition to helping you plan your research program, having a written research statement is handy when you are hired for that tenure-track position, because it is commonly used for tenure and promotion purposes and often incorporated into annual professional reviews.

An effective research statement accomplishes three key goals (Argow & Beane, 2009): (a) It clearly presents your scholarship in nonspecialist terms, (b) it places your research in a broader context (both scientifically and societally), and (c) it describes a plan for future accomplishments at the institution to which you are applying. Another way to think about the goal of your research statement is to consider whether, after reading it, a reader would be able to answer these questions: (a) What do you do (what is your field of study, what methods and techniques do you use, what are your major accomplishments)? (b) Why is your work important (why should both other scientists and nonscientists care, how have you contributed to your field)? (c) Where is your work going in the future (what are the next steps and how will you carry them out in your new job)?

To accomplish these goals, the three main components of the research statement that are typically recommended include an executive summary, a summary of your research field, and a summary of your own research (including past, current, and future plans). Organizationally, the summary of your research can be compiled using a chronological or topical outline. A chronological organization would comprise a summary of your research in the order in which it occurred, beginning with a project-by-project description of your graduate research from beginning to end and then any postdoctoral research, followed by future research plans. A topical organization of your research summary would comprise separate paragraphs or sections for each of your research interests by topic, with past, current, and future research on that topic included in each paragraph or section. This organizational approach is particularly useful if your research has several divergent topics; the sample research statement in Figure 4.1 generally takes this approach.

FIGURE 4.1

Russell B. Toomey, PhD
Statement of Research Interests

Sexual minority and ethnic minority youth disproportionately experience negative physical and mental health outcomes. My research interests can best be understood as an intersection between my desire to understand how contextual experiences of prejudice and discrimination influence adolescent well-being for minority populations (e.g., based on sexual orientation, ethnicity), the development of preventative interventions to reduce health disparities for these populations, and the use of advanced quantitative methodologies to answer complex questions. I find that these foci are not mutually exclusive; my focus on quantitative methodology allows me to answer substantive research questions in appropriate ways and then apply the results in the community, while advances in my quantitative knowledge and skill set allow me to pursue novel substantive research questions. In the following paragraphs I briefly discuss three specific areas of interest: (1) how contextual experiences and interpersonal relationships influence later health outcomes for vulnerable youth, (2) how engagement of vulnerable youth in extracurricular activities and civic engagement affects well-being, and (3) the use of advanced statistical methodologies in studying human development and the dynamic relationships that occur in adolescence.

Contextual and Interpersonal Influences on Health Outcomes

Ecological and life course models provide insight into the important role that context plays in human development. Beyond these metatheoretical models of human development, two theoretical frameworks have largely influenced my research on the disparate health outcomes of sexual and ethnic minority youth: the minority stress framework and social identity theory. Both of these frameworks suggest that the social context, including experiences of discrimination and bias-based victimization, help to explain the health disparities experienced by minority group members. My work in this area has concentrated on two populations: first, my doctoral training focused on the experiences of sexual minority (e.g., lesbian, gay, bisexual) and gender nonconforming youth (e.g., transgender), while my postdoctoral research is focused on ethnic minority youth (e.g., Latina/o youth). I sought to extend my expertise to ethnic minority youth in order to fill a gap in the literature that pays little attention to the complex interactions that occur between sexual and ethnic identities. My future research goal is to examine the complex intersectionality that exists between sexual orientation and ethnicity in order to develop a more nuanced understanding of the health disparities experienced by these populations.

Several studies provide insight into negative school-based experiences of LGBT youth (i.e., conclusive research suggests that sexual minority youth experience victimization at greater rates than heterosexual youth; Toomey, under review). Beyond documenting this risk, I am interested in the contextual and interpersonal *processes* that place these adolescents at risk and those that promote resilience. Using multilevel modeling (Toomey, McGuire, & Russell, 2011) and a mixed methods approach (McGuire, Anderson, Toomey, & Russell, 2010), my colleagues and I found that victimization based on gender nonconformity and sexual orientation is pervasive,

Example statement of research interests. Copyright 2011 by Russell B. Toomey. Printed with permission.

FIGURE 4.1 (*Continued*)

varies across schools, and that schools can implement specific policies and strategies to help make schools safer for these LGBT students. My recent work also documents that the association between adolescent gender nonconformity and young adult psychosocial maladjustment among LGBT individuals is largely accounted for by the experience of school victimization in adolescence (Toomey, Ryan, Diaz, Card, & Russell, 2010). In addition to school and peer contexts, I am also interested in family relationships of LGBT adolescents and the complex ecological interactions that can occur between families, schools, and the individual. My master's thesis explored sibling relationships of LGBT young adults (Toomey & Richardson, 2009), and I hope to explore these dynamic contextual experiences in my future research. For example, what protective role(s) do accepting siblings play in modifying associations between risk (e.g., school victimization) and well-being? My overarching research goal in this area is to understand the processes by which these contextual experiences influence adolescent and young adult well-being within the LGBT population and to ultimately develop culturally relevant preventative policies and interventions to help mitigate the negative effects of these experiences.

In the future, I plan to address the following research questions: (1) What are school-level (e.g., physical structure, school policies, teacher training) and interpersonal-level (e.g., teacher-student relationships) characteristics that promote well-being for adolescents who experience discrimination and bias-motivated victimization? (2) What are the dyadic and group related processes and characteristics that place LGBT and Latino youth at risk for disparate health outcomes? and (3) What are the dyadic and group related processes and characteristics that *promote* well-being for LGBT and Latino youth?

Extracurricular Activity and Civic Engagement of Minority Youth

The past 30 years of research provides convincing evidence that LGBT youth are at risk for disparate health outcomes. Meyer's (2002) minority stress model provides a way to conceptualize how youth experience minority stress related to a LGBT identity and provides for the possibility that social networks and coping strategies can modify the association between negative experiences and health outcomes. School-based extracurricular activity engagement of adolescents is one protective factor that has been identified in the general adolescent literature; my dissertation work extended this literature to include a focus on LGBT youth.

I recently collaborated on a chapter that examined LGBT youths' involvement in gay-straight alliances (GSAs) and socio-political involvement in a Queer Youth Advocacy Day event (Russell, Toomey, Crockett, & Laub, 2010). Our chapter reviews the literature on civic engagement, builds on a theoretical framework of youth civic engagement proposed by Flanagan (2004), and examines the frequency of participation in LGBT-related social activism activities. We find that students involved in LGBT-specific social justice activities plan to continue engaging in LGBT-related advocacy. I expanded on this initial documentation of involvement in my dissertation and found that school-based extracurricular activities serve as a protective factor for sexual minority youth in that they promote greater school connectedness, which in turn is associated with later well-being (Toomey & Russell, 2011, revise / resubmit). I also documented that Gay-Straight Alliances are associated with academic achievement and well-being for LGBT students (Toomey & Russell, 2011; Toomey, Ryan, Diaz, & Russell, 2011). In the future, I hope to extend these school-based investigations to examine LGBT adolescent experiences in youth development organizations and to include attention to ethnic minority issues related to extracurricular and civic engagement.

Advanced Statistical Methodologies

In part, my interest in advanced statistical methodologies is rooted in being able to answer the questions posed in my substantive research agenda. Additionally, as I continually learn about new quantitative methods and advances in those methods I am able to ask novel research questions. My experience and expertise can be categorized in three areas: structural equation modeling, longitudinal methods, and interdependent data analysis.

Example statement of research interests.

FIGURE 4.1 (*Continued*)

My interest in structural equation modeling (SEM) as a powerful tool was sparked when I learned about advantages of this approach over traditional statistical methods. In my research, I have utilized SEM to examine traditional path models and to examine mean and covariance structures models (MACS; Toomey, Ryan, Diaz, Card, & Russell, 2010). I have also utilized SEM to examine the psychometric properties of a new measure of adolescent coping that is specific to lesbian, gay, bisexual, and transgender (LGBT) adolescents (Toomey, Ryan, Diaz, & Russell, in preparation). In the future, I plan to address questions of contextual influences using multilevel SEM, an emerging use of SEM.

As a researcher who is focused on understanding development across the life course, I am also interested in how to model longitudinal data. I utilized longitudinal SEM methods (e.g., cross-lagged panel modeling) in my dissertation to answer questions about the long-term effects of adolescent extracurricular activity involvement using the *National Longitudinal Study of Adolescent Health*. In addition to SEM, I also have the knowledge base to use multilevel modeling (MLM) to model multivariate growth trajectories between discrimination and ethnic identity development (specifically, growth curve analysis; Toomey, Umaña-Taylor, Updegraff, & Jahromi, in preparation).

My substantive area often deals with other types of interdependent data (e.g., disentangling person-level experiences from characteristics of schools). To deal with the problem of interdependence, I have utilized MLM to model individual- and school-level contextual effects in a paper that examines how school-level policies and programs are associated with students' perceptions of safety for gender nonconforming peers (Toomey, McGuire, & Russell, 2011). Extending beyond the focus of MLM, I coauthored a chapter on the use and future directions of the social relations model to model more complex interdependencies in groups (Card & Toomey, 2011).

Example statement of research interests.

Executive Summary

Your first paragraph should operate like an abstract, presenting the basic information about your research program that search committees are interested in during the early, screening phase of the review process (J. Austin, 2002). Think of it this way: If the reader were to stop reading after the first paragraph, what essential information would you want to make sure had been delivered in that paragraph? You should include clearly stated research goals, the most compelling motivation behind your research questions, and the general approach you intend to take to answer these questions. As a result, the executive summary should answer these questions: What is my area of research? Why is my research important? What are my long-term research goals? In the sample research statement in Figure 4.1, the first paragraph provides an example of a concise overview of a research program. It is also important to adapt this paragraph to fit the job description by briefly stating how your research will fit with, contribute to, and be feasible within the institution to which you are applying. For example, if you are applying for a position as a comparative psychologist, but your research statement never mentions that you have worked with animals or plan to work with animals, the search committee may consider this omission in determining that you are not the most suitable candidate for the position.

Your Research Field

After the initial executive summary paragraph, you should provide a brief description of your general area of research. Define the broad problem domain of your research and emphasize why it is an important area of inquiry. In other words, why does your research matter? If it is a well-known area, identify what you think is the primary question and its merit. If it is a new or underdeveloped research domain, support the need for this new area. If possible, tie the importance of this domain to the specific job description of the faculty position. You should describe your research area in broad and inclusive terms so it can be viewed as both relevant and unrestrictive. It can be useful to mention several key figures in your field and what these scholars have done, what they are doing, and how your research fits in with and extends their work. However, it is generally agreed that there is no need to include an extensive literature review or a long list of references (J. Austin, 2002). Rather, the purpose of this general overview is to place your work in the context of other scholars and describe how it addresses the gaps in the current literature. In the sample research statement in Figure 4.1, the author uses the first paragraphs of each section to orient the reader to how his research topic connects with theoretical perspectives on health disparities among his populations of interest and past research on minority stress.

This section will also show that you have a deep knowledge of your research area and could teach or collaborate in the area. Remember that the members of the search committee are likely not experts in your field, so you are not writing to impress them with your deep and nuanced understanding of your area of research. Rather, you are writing to succinctly and clearly define your field of study. This particular component is often left out of research statements but can be more important than your own results that you present later.

Summary of Your Research

Having covered your general area of research, you then have the opportunity to explain how your current research is poised to open up a new line of inquiry and knowledge. At this point in the document, you should specifically state how your research is contributing to the problem domain you identified in the previous paragraph. You should take the opportunity here to be passionate and to describe what is particularly exciting about your own research, emphasizing how your research is moving the field forward. Search committees, chairs, deans, and college presidents want to hire people who will make a difference, and you have to convince them that you will indeed be making a difference.

The beginning of this section is also a good place for you to include a general discussion of the research methodologies and approaches you use. What research methods are you comfortable with, and how are they important to understanding your research questions? What expertise do you have? This is not the time to be shy or timid. Academics do have to promote themselves from time to time, which may be especially difficult given the typical intellectual culture of academia. To do so appropriately, think of the volleyball serve analogy: You have to demonstrate your competence and expertise strongly enough to serve the ball over the net but not be so overconfident that you make it go out of bounds. A trusted mentor or peers going through this same process should be able to provide guidance about the accuracy of your "serve."

As you expand this section of the research statement either chronologically or topically, review your research progress to date. The sample research statement in Figure 4.1 offers an excellent example of how to briefly summarize and integrate past research projects throughout the body of the statement. It is useful to refer to your past and current publications and presentations (listed in American Psychological Association format) as appropriate when describing your research. Rather than simply providing a list of your publications, describe the accomplishments of each paper or project with clear statements explaining what you did and what its significance is; that is, provide a brief annotation. As with your coverage of your research area, be specific but avoid including details that will confuse or overwhelm someone who is not an expert in the field. For each paper you describe, ask yourself what contribution it made to the literature, and convey this in your statement.

The committee wants to know that you have had a positive impact on the field (or that you have a potential impact). You do not need to focus only on your most current research; instead, try to present a unifying story or trajectory driving your training and past research (Ting, 2008). Linking your projects conceptually is a useful way to present a unifying story. Huang-Pollock and Mikami (2007) suggested the following formula: "I did study X and found that . . . so, I got interested in question Z . . . which led me to conduct this other study, in which I found . . . " (p. 104). This section can also detail upcoming projects, which are especially worth mentioning if you have preliminary data.

Throughout your review of your research contributions, it is particularly important that you incorporate and emphasize the uniqueness of your "problem" and the approach you take to examine it. What is novel about your research? This may appear obvious to you, but it usually is not obvious to those reading your research statement. A secondary but similarly important function of promoting the uniqueness of your research is to show the committee that you understand the concept of novel research. However, be sure to focus on your work's contributions to your field of study, not on your personal research experience and skills. J. Austin (2002) reminded us that "a research plan should tell how great the science is, not how great you are" (para. 56). Again, the sample statement in Figure 4.1 expertly integrates discussion of the relevance, importance, and originality of the applicant's research, establishing the contributions he has already made in the field and that he is poised to continue doing so with his line of research.

Your Future Goals and Research Plans

Once you have described your past and current research, it is important to report specific future research plans; the fourth paragraph of the sample research statement in Figure 4.1 provides a good example of this. It is common to include broad research goals that cover the implications of your research and how these goals relate to where the field is likely heading in the next 2 to 10 years. Continue to focus on how your work is going to contribute something interesting, vital, and new to the field. Next, you should provide an overview for each proposed research area, including specific projects for the next year and the next 3–5 year period. For example, have you identified a critical question and a methodology for answering it? What are your major hypotheses? What results would be exciting? Your proposed research plan should follow logically from the research you have already outlined in your statement, and it should be feasible, given your experience and expertise (Ting, 2008). Organizationally, you can provide your future research goals and plans in a single section at the end of your research statement, or you can describe them at the end of each individual section of your various research areas.

It is especially important to use this section of your research statement to convey your independence as a researcher. "Completing my dissertation" is not an appropriate future research goal. Although your research plans should build on your prior experience, they should not be direct extensions of your advisor's work. This is particularly important if your current publications are mostly (or solely) published with your advisor. The committee needs to see that you have independent ideas and can meet the challenge of establishing your own research lab. Proposing and substantiating the value of a specific set of research projects will help convince the committee of your ability to make the transition from graduate student (or postdoctoral student) to faculty member. Many students may not be convinced of their ability to make the transition to the role of independent researcher and thus have a hard time providing concrete plans for future research. As a student, the goal is often to finish the project at hand and think about future projects later. If this is the case for you, it might help you to construct a research statement as an act of professional development and as an opportunity to spend some time developing future research plans (with the knowledge that they are not meant to be set in stone).

Several additional considerations for this section include making sure your plan is realistic, potentially fundable, open to collaboration, and tailored to the institution. First, make sure you give specifics about how you will effect your plan, such as by presenting preliminary data to support the viability of your projects. It is worthwhile to present more than one good idea. Even the best idea might fail to pan out, so you should have at least one backup. Second, you should identify any funding organizations that are likely to support your research plans. If you have any experience with proposal writing or past funding, mention it here. Schwebel and Karver (2004) stated that successful applicants "show the ability to receive grants by funding dissertation or postdoctoral research through small (or even large) extramural grants and demonstrate plans for a research program that will soon be fundable through extramural grants" (p. 175). Third, if you can identify faculty or research groups with whom you could collaborate at the institution to which you are applying, or facilities there that you could make use of, highlight these in a closing paragraph. Your aim is to convince the search committee that you will both strengthen existing research at the institution and spawn new and exciting research directions. This last point will also emphasize that you have researched the targeted institution and have customized your materials beyond the common "one-size-fits-all" approach, another way to make you to stand out from the applicant crowd.

Logistics

It is generally acknowledged that a research statement should be written in prose (not bulleted) but with useful and easily visible headings. There is no single appropriate length for a research statement; the length depends on your record of research and the conventions in your field. Ultimately, you should state what needs to be stated in a clear and organized way. Most sources (e.g., J. Austin, 2002; Career Services, University of Pennsylvania, n.d.; Stanford Career Development Center, 2004) agree that a research statement should be between one and five pages long, with two to three pages being the most common recommendation. Shorter statements (one to three pages) can be single spaced, but for longer ones (four to five pages) 1.5 spacing is recommended.

Regardless of length, it is important to write as clearly and concisely as you can. Remember that your research statement is also a writing sample. Keep your audience in mind (i.e., busy faculty members) and recognize that it is possible they will be skimming your application materials. Also remember that the people reading your statement will not be specialists in your field, so it is particularly important to avoid overly technical or specialized language. Make sure your mentors and trusted colleagues read and reread your research statement before you send it to the search committee.

CUSTOMIZING YOUR STATEMENT TO THE POSITION

There is no secret formula for writing a research statement. Each statement must uniquely reflect the nature of your research, your level of experience and expertise, and the type of institution to which you are applying. If you are applying to several different types of positions, you will likely need several versions of your research statement. When applying to top-tier research universities, your research statement should ideally demonstrate that you will bring unique and critical expertise, grant opportunities, and potential for high productivity to the institution. It can be particularly beneficial to explain how your proposed research program broadens, strengthens, and complements the current faculty's programs of research. The research statement is of particular importance to doctoral institutions (Clifton & Buskist, 2005).

Liberal arts colleges often expect a balance between teaching and research; therefore, when writing a research statement for these positions you should include examples of how students have been or will be involved in your research program (indeed, many colleges will specifically request this in their advertisement). For example, it can be useful to discuss what kinds of tasks students would complete and what kinds of projects they would work on, including what experiences they would acquire. These types of topics should be included when you are applying for positions at institutions that do not have graduate programs and where attractive candidates will involve undergraduates in their research programs (Argow & Beane, 2009). Research projects that involve improvements to student learning would certainly be of interest to teaching-oriented institutions, including liberal arts and community colleges.

Beyond the research and teaching climate of the institution, carefully consider the characteristics of the institution to which you are applying and tailor your research statement to correspond with the institution's resources and needs. Your research statement should propose a plan of research that is compatible with the opportunities available at each institution to which you are applying. Teaching-oriented institutions may have different institutional resources and facilities than doctoral institutions and may also have higher teaching loads (Argow & Beane, 2009). If specific research specialties are listed in the job advertisement, be sure to address how your work corresponds to what the department is seeking.

PREPARING TO SUBMIT YOUR APPLICATION: FEEDBACK AND PROOFREADING

Careful proofreading and seeking feedback are integral aspects of dossier preparation. In addition to reviewing the document yourself, have other people read your statement as well. Ask your advisor, junior faculty members, and former graduate student colleagues to look it over. It is helpful to have your document read by individuals familiar with your research and within your research area, as well as by those with other research specialties. Seek feedback from individuals currently working at the types of institutions at which you hope to work, particularly if they are different from your current institution. In seeking feedback, be sure to ask for specific guidance from each reader. For example, to ensure that the information you are presenting is clear, it could be useful to ask a reader whether he or she could read your statement and quickly present a 5-minute summary. Similarly, you could also ask other reviewers to report in their own words after reading your statement why they view your research as important and exciting. In addition to reading your statement for content, fellow graduate students and family or friends may also catch any typographical or grammatical errors.

Research statements typically require ongoing review and revision, so it is important to start early in order to have time to process new information between drafts. Remember to get feedback along the way from friends, colleagues, and mentors. It can be helpful to read other people's statements, identify specifically what you like or dislike about them, and then choose an appropriate format for you. You can ask to look over copies of the research statements of friends and colleagues who have had successful job searches, or you could ask junior faculty members in your department whether they would be willing to share theirs. Remember to proofread carefully and continually, and ask a colleague or mentor to review your statement before you send it out (Ting, 2008).

SELECTING ACCOMPANYING WRITING SAMPLES

The majority of job postings for assistant professor positions include requests for reprints, papers, or writing samples as part of the application (Clifton & Buskist, 2005). Usually, the posting will ask for a specific number of reprints or stipulate a type of document to include with your application. Be sure to follow these directions carefully. If an advertisement does not request writing samples, it is typically not recommended to send them in unsolicited (Woolf, 2010). If a job advertisement asks for an article, essay, or dissertation or book chapter of no more than 30 pages, make sure you stay within the page limit. One option could be to make necessary cuts to your documents and then offer to make electronic versions of the complete documents available to search committee members as well.

The writing sample can provide a significant measure of a candidate's intellectual ability, research potential, and eventual likelihood of receiving tenure. Thus, it is typically best to send in published rather than unpublished work. However, you should send the strongest and most appropriate writing sample you have to offer that is relevant to the specific job in question, even if it is an unpublished chapter or essay. In general, an article on which you are first author and which is published article in a high-quality, peer-reviewed journal is your best option. Because most new doctorates do not have those kinds of publications, you may be submitting all your papers, including publications on which you are second author. If you do not have any published or in-press articles, you can send a manuscript you are currently working on (if it has been adequately revised), a master's thesis, or portions of a qualifying paper or research papers from graduate courses. You can also send portions of your dissertation. If you opt to do the latter, it is preferable to include a later chapter that shows the results of your research rather than a review of the literature. Regardless of which papers you chose to include, it is helpful if you have also referred to these papers in your research statement to contextualize them within your broader research program and/or goals (Baron, 2001).

Teaching Statements

Also known as a *teaching philosophy* or a *statement of teaching interests*, the *teaching statement* is a purposeful and reflective essay about your teaching beliefs and practices. In other words, this statement is an individual narrative that includes not only your beliefs about the teaching and learning process but also concrete examples of the ways in which you exhibit these beliefs in the classroom. Whereas many applications might ask for a teaching statement, the value that is placed on this document is likely to vary considerably. At larger, research-oriented schools, the teaching statement may rarely be a deciding factor in the hiring process, whereas it may hold greater significance at smaller, private, liberal arts colleges. Regardless of how seriously the committee considers your statement, at some point in the search process you will be expected to discuss your teaching in a thoughtful and coherent manner. Having prepared this document will help you accomplish that task (Montell, 2003), even if the document is not formally requested by a search committee. Exhibit 4.1 describes the most important characteristics of the teaching statement.

EXHIBIT 4.1

What the Literature Says . . . About the Most Important Characteristics of a Teaching Statement

---

O'Neal, Meizlish, and Kaplan (2007) surveyed search committee members, asking them to rank the most important characteristics of a teaching statement. The results revealed that the top characteristics of a good teaching statement include the following:

- evidence of practice, including specific examples of how theory is linked with actual teaching experiences;
- evidence that the applicant is student centered and attuned to differences in student ability, learning style, or level, including specific evidence of methods of instruction and assessment that go beyond traditional lecture and testing methodology and that address the diversity of the student body;
- evidence of reflectiveness, including specific examples of struggles with instructional challenges and how they were resolved, and an outline for future development as a teacher;
- evidence of a value for teaching; for example, a tone or language that communicates enthusiasm for teaching and a consideration of it that is on par with research pursuits; and
- prose that is well written, clear, and readable.

Conversely, the two top characteristics of an unsuccessful teaching statement included

- being generic, full of boilerplate language, and not offering evidence of serious effort or thought; and
- providing no specific evidence or examples of practice.

O'Neal et al. (2007) also provided a rubric to assess teaching statements in the following five areas:

- *Goals for student learning.* What knowledge, skills, and attitudes are important for student success in your discipline? What are you preparing students for? What are key challenges in the teaching–learning process?
- *Enactment of goals (teaching methods).* What teaching methods do you use? How do these methods contribute to your goals for students? Why are these methods appropriate for use in your discipline?
- *Assessment of goals (measuring student learning).* How do you know your goals for students are being met? What sorts of assessment tools do you use (e.g., tests, papers, portfolios, journals) and why? How do assessments contribute to student learning? How do assessments communicate disciplinary priorities?
- *Creating an inclusive learning environment.* How do your own and your students' identities (e.g., race, gender, class), background, experience, and levels of privilege affect the classroom? How do you account for diverse learning styles? How do you integrate diverse perspectives into your teaching?
- *Structure, rhetoric, and language.* How is the reader engaged? Is the language used appropriate to the discipline? How is the statement thematically structured?

PURPOSE AND COMMON COMPONENTS

Like the research statement, a teaching statement has several purposes. It is likely that your primary reason for first writing a teaching statement was that it was requested from a potential employer. In addition to being a common component of a job application, it is also frequently used for tenure and promotion purposes or for teaching awards (Weimer, 2010). Prospective and current employers and colleagues will read your statement to assess your understanding of the value and purpose of teaching and learning. A teaching statement can demonstrate that you have been reflective about your teaching, and it can give you a forum to communicate your goals as an instructor and to describe your teaching activities that correspond to those goals. Indeed, it has been suggested that the actual philosophy you express is not as important as demonstrating to the committee that you have given the matter enough thought to have developed a philosophy that you are able to express in a clear and meaningful way (R. N. Austin, 2006).

Second, as with constructing a research statement, writing a teaching statement is an opportunity for self-reflection, with the goal of improving your teaching. In this sense, it can act as a personal mission statement. Indeed, taking time to consider one's goals, actions, and vision provides an opportunity for development that can be personally and professionally enriching. Reviewing and revising former statements of teaching philosophy can help teachers to reflect on their growth and renew their dedication to the instructional goals and values they hold. If your campus has a center for the advancement of teaching and learning, it can be useful to attend relevant workshops or meet individually with staff or affiliated faculty to develop and refine your philosophy of teaching, as well as your written teaching statement.

The teaching statement should not simply include a list of courses you have taught; it should not be a review of your teaching experiences listed in your CV. Instead, focus on your teaching values, goals, and practices. Make your teaching statement a personal narrative that includes "your conception of teaching and learning, a description of how you teach, and justification for why you teach that way" (S. L. Smith, 2007, para. 1). It is an opportunity to explain to the search committee what you actually do in the classroom, so you should explain your specific disciplinary context and use specific examples of your practice or things you have done in the classroom. It can also be useful to keep a broad definition of *teaching* in mind: For example, informal interactions with students during office hours or supervising teaching assistants or clinical supervision can be discussed.

Although there is no fixed formula for the teaching statement, it typically includes five standard elements: your teaching values, goals, pedagogy, methods of assessment, and professional development as a teacher.

Values

Use the first paragraph to show your commitment to teaching. Why is teaching important to you? How do you want to make a difference in the lives of your students? What do you find rewarding about teaching? What inspires you to keep teaching in the face of challenges or difficulties? A sample teaching statement produced by Jessica Irons when she was a graduate student at Auburn University is shown in Figure 4.2. The statement begins with several sentences that convey her passion for teaching and what she generally hopes students gain from having her as an instructor. The beginning of the statement is also an appropriate place to include an account of how you value diversity as an instructor, including a discussion of diverse ways of learning. If you are having difficulty getting started, you could use the card-sorting activity outlined by Beatty, Leigh, and Dean (2009) to see how your beliefs about education are related to five fundamental philosophies of education. Although you can do this activity individually, it can be particularly useful to do it with some of your peers.

Goals

In addition to establishing your values about and commitment to teaching, it is important to provide your goals for teaching in your discipline. These goals should include content objectives but also emphasize the skills you hope students will learn by the end of your class. You may also want to acknowledge the broader educational or life lessons you want your students to acquire as well. The author of our sample teaching statement in Figure 4.2 describes her goals throughout the body of her statement, covering outcomes such as critical thinking and real-world application of knowledge. To determine these goals, it can be helpful to start with your learning objectives or outcomes (both in general and for particular courses). Furthermore, if you start your statement by describing your teaching objectives, "the rest of your philosophy statement can then support these objectives which should be achievable and relevant to your teaching practices" (Haugen, 1998, para. 2).

If you have not had much practice developing teaching objectives, there are a variety of ways to extend your goals beyond simply hoping students learn the fundamental content of the courses you teach. For example, Haugen (1998) encouraged teachers to consider the following types of questions:

> Do you hope to foster critical thinking, facilitate the acquisition
> of life-long learning skills, or develop problem-solving strategies?
> What is your role in orienting students to what it means to be
> an educated person in your field? In what specific ways do you

FIGURE 4.2

Teaching Statement
Jessica Irons

To love something truly, as I love psychology, is gratifying. To share that love is even more rewarding. Teaching allows me to share my love for psychology with hope that I may inspire others to develop a similar passion. By showing excitement for the subject matter and bringing relevant, real-world examples into the classroom, I try to show students how psychological principles work in their lives. By teaching the scientific method, I teach students how to question systematically the world around them, including information taught in the classroom. When I teach I demand excellence and nurture students' abilities to achieve that excellence.

Many of my teaching techniques are borrowed from past teachers. For example, when beginning each class, I recap quickly what was covered previously so that any questions can be addressed, as much information is cumulative. In addition to review, this recap provides students the opportunity to continue to reflect about the relevance of psychology to their own experiences. I remind students of how much they have learned thus far and guide them to new revelations rather than giving them answers. By offering praise for class participation, students feel comfortable participating and offering their insights into how they find psychology relates to, and affects, their lives.

In addition to learning how psychology relates to life experiences, I hope my students will become critical thinkers in both everyday life and in academic pursuits. By relating material to the real-world whenever possible, I can better engage students with content. I can also encourage students to examine critically the world around them while considering how psychological principles fit into their unique experiences and the experiences of others. It is not uncommon to hear me say, "Now, why is this important?" One important aspect of my teaching that becomes important for encouraging critical thinking has been my successful establishment of rapport. If I have provided a safe place for students to be critical of the information they are learning (and learned in the past), then students will be more likely to think critically. Despite all efforts, there are also the few students who resent being asked to think critically. I must always remember that I can lead a student to knowledge but I cannot make him think. My job is to lead well.

Although I believe that real-world application of material is essential for student success, I do not discount the importance of knowledge for its own sake. Some principles may not be applicable to students' lives, so we (I and my students) must find other ways to make the information meaningful. Some material is made clearer and can be recalled better when conveyed through analogies or hands-on demonstrations. However difficult the task may be, as a teacher I must find ways to bring the students closer to understanding the material. One technique that promises to make the material relevant, at least in the classroom, is to teach students to *use* the psychological principles they are learning about to help improve their skills for learning and retention. For example, when I teach about stress and coping I share ways to improve coping skills—a necessary set of skills for any student. Also, when I teach students about learning principles, I teach them how to set up study reinforcement schedules to help them prepare for exams. If a student uses good coping skills and effectively sets up contingencies with which to reinforce good study habits then the content material will be easier to learn—relevant to their lives or not.

To assess how well I have accomplished my teaching goals, I seek frequent feedback from my students. My goals for students are largely for them to become critical thinkers, to utilize psychological principles in their own lives, and to appreciate knowledge for its own sake. If students have demonstrated the achievement of these goals through classroom participation or graded efforts perhaps I have done my job well. If feedback from students reflects that they have learned and enjoyed the material, then I know I have created an environment conducive to student learning in which successfully achieved some key learning objectives. It is important to inform my teaching both after the teaching experience (the end of the course) and as the process is ongoing such that I can make improvements to benefit student learning. If I can become a better teacher, my students will become better learners, which is, after all, the most important opportunity for which students can expect from the educational experience.

Example teaching statement. Copyright 2011 by Jessica Irons. Printed with permission.

want to improve the education of students in your field? . . . Are
there discussions in academic journals or in professional organizations about shortcomings in the education of students today
or unmet needs in the discipline[,] and do you have ideas about
how to address those shortcomings and needs? (para. 2)

In addition to addressing one or more of these queries, also remember
not to ignore your research. One way of bringing your research activities into your teaching statement is to discuss how you integrate your
research and teaching; this can be accomplished by explaining how you
advance your field through teaching (O'Neal, Meizlish, & Kaplan, 2007).

Pedagogy

Having laid out the goals you have for your students, discuss the methods you use to work toward those objectives. How do you conduct your
classes? What types of in-class activities and assignments do you use,
and what do they ask students to do? The goal is to include teaching
strategies and methods to help people "see" you in the classroom and
to help your readers create an image in their minds of the learning
environment you create for your students. You should explain the specific techniques, strategies, and exercises you have used or plan to use
in your classes. Discuss choices you make about content, course readings, assignments, and delivery. For example, do you mainly lecture
or predominantly use active learning methods? Do you give multiple
choice exams or essays? Do students complete individual or collaborative projects?

Once you have provided your learning objectives (or goals), it is
important to explicitly connect these pedagogical approaches with
your teaching objectives and describe how each practice is designed
to enhance each objective. For example, if you use active learning or
student-centered learning principles, explain why you use these techniques and discuss how they increase learning among your students.
The sample teaching statement in Figure 4.2 is an excellent example
of how to combine a discussion of your teaching goals and pedagogical techniques. Throughout her statement, the author describes broader
techniques (e.g., establishing rapport with her students to facilitate
participation) and more specific techniques (e.g., setting up study reinforcement schedules to teach about learning principles) in relation to
different teaching goals. You also should relate the decisions you make
about course structure and methods to the kinds of classes you teach
(e.g., large lecture, general education requirement, small discussion,
lab). You do not teach every class in the same way, so be sure to explain
how you alter your teaching techniques on the basis of the topic, level of
the course, and number of students in the class (Lang, 2010). If you have

experience managing a diverse classroom, working with first-generation college students, or teaching effective online courses, use specific examples from these experiences to explain your pedagogy. If you can, whenever possible, relate your methods to national-level needs for teaching in your discipline. Notice that these elements focus on how you and your students engage with course material instead of emphasizing course texts and topics or generic disciplinary complexities.

If you have little experience teaching, you can draw on your experiences as a student in a variety of classes. You have likely been the recipient of both bad and good teaching and have developed some opinions about what does and what does not work. You can also draw on your experiences as a teaching assistant. In this position, you probably encountered some difficulties or frustrations as well as ideas and techniques that yielded positive results. In your teaching statement, you can explain these situations and discuss how you addressed them or applied the effective practices in your own classroom. A transformative personal experience—the undergraduate research experience—can be worth mentioning; write about how you hope to provide your students with a similar opportunity (University of California, Berkeley, Career Center, 2011). Overall, reflect on the life experiences you have had that have affected how you think about teaching. For example, how do the lessons you have learned from your own experiences affect the kind of classes that you would like to teach or the kind of teacher you would like to be?

You can also use this opportunity to write about the courses you would like to teach. Remember, this should be specific to the institution, so some research into the institution to which you are applying would be helpful. What courses are already being offered that you might teach? What new courses might you bring to the department? Contact the head of the search committee if you have questions about the teaching expectations for the position. It is particularly important that you do not present a limited range of classes. For example, do not list only graduate courses or advanced undergraduate courses as your teaching interests. In addition, keep in mind that involving undergraduates in research, mentoring, and advising are all types of teaching you can include as "courses" of interest. Be sure to research the positions for which you are applying. Do not describe graduate courses you might teach and then send your teaching statement to an undergraduate-only department. Customization matters: Make sure all the application materials are appropriate for the position for which you are applying. It is also important not to make unrealistic promises to devote too much time and energy to teaching, especially during the first few years. Unrealistic plans to meet individually with student every week, for example, will not be helpful for your application.

Assessment

Having clarified your goals and the teaching practices you use to achieve them, the next step is to explain how you assess students' learning. In terms of a student's behavior, how would you describe the ideal outcome of your courses? What skills should the student have on completion of a course? For example, if one of your teaching objectives is to develop problem-solving skills, then it makes sense to assess your students' ability to solve problems. In that case, "discuss how you construct problems for them to solve, what skills those problems are meant to evaluate, and the level of performance that you are seeking" (Haugan, 1998, para. 9). You can also consider assessment in terms of measuring your effectiveness as an instructor and discuss it with regard to professional development. The author of the sample teaching statement in Figure 4.2 uses the last paragraph to discuss evaluating student learning as well as improving her own teaching.

Professional Development

One of the most important qualities a teacher can exhibit is a willingness to learn and adapt. An open mind shows that what you can become as a teacher is not limited by what you already are. If you indicate these qualities in your teaching statement, search committees are more likely to view you as a viable long-term employee (R. N. Austin, 2006). Use this section of your teaching statement to discuss what steps you have already taken to improve your teaching (e.g., classes, workshops, conferences, readings) and what you plan to do to continue improving your teaching once hired. Because it is important not to sound overconfident about teaching, this is an appropriate place to discuss areas of weakness and how you plan to address them.

Logistics

The general guidelines for a teaching statement include keeping it brief and well-written. Although teaching statements are usually about three to five pages long when submitted for tenure and promotion purposes, those included in job applications are typically one to two pages long. They are usually written using a first-person, present-tense narrative approach, and the style is usually reflective and personal (The McGraw Center for Teaching and Learning, 2010). One of the most common pitfalls of teaching statements is reliance on abstract educational catchphrases that do not convey information about who the applicant is as an instructor. These types of statements may be perceived as disingenuous. The best way to avoid overly generic statements is to provide concrete examples of practices you have used, or anticipate using, that can illustrate your ideas and help the reader visualize you in the classroom. Also keep in mind that committee members reviewing your application for a faculty position are reading dozens or hundreds of these documents. Thus, think about what is going to set you apart and how are you going to ensure that they remember you as an extraordinary teacher. "What brings a teaching philosophy to life is the extent to which it creates a vivid portrait of a person who is intentional about teaching practices and committed to his/her career" (University Center for the Advancement of Teaching, 2009, para. 12).

CUSTOMIZING YOUR STATEMENT TO THE POSITION

A teaching statement is typically emphasized as an important element of your application package at baccalaureate and master's institutions (Benson & Buskist, 2005; Clifton & Buskist, 2005); these types of institutions are likely to request statements of teaching philosophy and teaching evaluations about twice as often as doctoral institutions. However, even though teaching statements may not serve as the primary mechanism for selecting finalists at predominantly research-oriented institutions, they nonetheless may serve as a filter in the early stages of the hiring process or may become more important in later decision-making stages when the committee is attempting to select between a small group of highly qualified candidates. Thus, no matter what type (or types) of institutions to which are you applying, you should take the time to carefully tailor your teaching statement to the position and institution. As with cover letters, a generic teaching statement could be an easy reason for search committee members to reject your application.

From the Trenches—Employer Experiences and Advice

I'm chair of psychology at a small liberal arts school which emphasizes teaching. I expect candidates to address their applications to our specific needs and values. There should be a clear commitment to a career with a teaching emphasis. There should be an understanding of the purpose of liberal arts education. Teaching experience is useful, especially if it is in a liberal arts setting. Constructive reflection on their teaching experience, some integration of current teaching methods, and some evidence of attempts to act on feedback and improve the course each time it is taught is highly desirable. A well-thought-out Statement of Teaching Philosophy is a plus. We are looking for much more than an impressive research record.

—Stephen C., PhD in experimental psychology, professor at Samford University

If you are applying to a wide range of schools with varying emphases on teaching, you may find it easiest to write multiple versions of your statement. Some schools want evidence that you will be a good teacher but that you do not spend too much of your time on teaching. Others want to know that you truly care about teaching and that your research productivity is directly linked to your teaching endeavors. Overall, it is a good idea to talk a little about supporting students in your research statement and to briefly discuss your research in your teaching statement; the extent and tenor with which you do this will depend on the type of school to which you are applying. In your teaching statement, you may also want to address the specific aspects of a position that are explicitly mentioned in the advertisement for it.

Even if your teaching philosophy stays the same, your teaching style will likely vary depending on the institution. Therefore, if you are applying to various types of institutions—community colleges, liberal arts colleges, and state universities—you may need to write several different statements that stress different aspects of your teaching experience and techniques. There are several different ways to gather information to help you decide how to amend your teaching statement. Before you start writing, look closely at the job advertisement and the institution's website. Find out how large the institution is and what the institution values. It can be useful to look at the mission statement of the department, college, or university. The information you glean from this research can determine what aspects of your teaching philosophy and experience to highlight. You will need some information about typical class sizes so that you can appropriately describe your abilities for teaching large or small courses. For example, emphasizing your abilities to command lecture-based courses filled with several hundred students may not be beneficial in an application to a liberal arts college but could be essential in an application to a larger state university (Montell, 2003). Smaller schools are likely to be more interested in your ability to teach small sections and provide on-on-one assistance or mentorship to students. Ultimately, the search committee will not only be looking for experience in teaching the types of classes they offer but also an understanding of what is expected of an instructor at their institution.

Regardless of where you are applying to, the primary objective of your teaching statement is to demonstrate that you are committed to teaching and that you consider it a vital element of your role as a faculty member. The majority of faculty positions require teaching, which means that being a committed teacher will necessarily be regarded positively both during the hiring process and in ongoing evaluations. Obviously, teaching ability matters to different degrees at different institutions. However, "even at institutions where the tenure decision will ultimately rest on grants received and papers published, being a good and committed teacher is necessary to make the probationary period go smoothly" (R. N. Austin, 2006, para. 5).

PREPARING TO SUBMIT YOUR APPLICATION: FEEDBACK AND PROOFREADING

As with your other documents, starting early and seeking ongoing feedback are necessary. Once you are almost finished, it is particularly important to review your teaching statement for potential misinterpretations. Unfortunately, it is sometimes possible that a sentence you believe clearly conveys your intentions suggests something different to members of a search committee. For example, a strong statement conveying beliefs about what makes a good teacher might be interpreted as the candidate not being open to other perspectives. A statement of your preferences for teaching certain classes might be taken to mean that you have no interest in teaching anything else. Ultimately, your goal should be to "find a balance between making a clear statement that might make you sound too rigid and making an overly vague statement that makes you sound cooperative but without vision" (Grundman, 2006, p. 1332)—think the volleyball serve analogy.

The best way to detect these problems is to have others read your statement and summarize what they think it says. At this point, you might want to solicit input from friends outside your discipline as well as from your peers and from faculty members with whom you are comfortable. If there is a center for teaching and learning on your campus, it can also be useful to solicit feedback from someone there. Be sure to give yourself time between revisions so that you can get some distance from the statement and view it with a more objective eye. It is also helpful to have one last set of eyes proofread it for you before you send it out.

Teaching Portfolios

In addition to the teaching statement, it is not uncommon for institutions to ask for information beyond that which is typically covered in a CV (i.e., the courses you have taught and are prepared to teach). A teaching portfolio can serve this purpose. Although it can take many forms and vary significantly in length, in essence, a teaching portfolio is a thoughtfully prepared collection of materials that demonstrates your teaching strengths and accomplishments. The portfolio is not meant to be exhaustive; instead, the aim is to be representative of various aspects of your teaching. This is not limited to what you do in the classroom; rather, a portfolio should also provide evidence of teaching activities such as planning and amending courses on the basis of feedback, assessing student learning, advising or mentoring students (in office hours or in larger projects such as theses and dissertations), supervising student research, and participating in professional development. If you have been highly involved in teaching, it can also include published articles on teaching and learning, teaching awards and certificates, and evidence of experience with curriculum development and assessment.

When a teaching portfolio is requested with your initial application, it is important to refer to your teaching interests and experiences in your cover letter and then refer the reader to your portfolio (in addition to your teaching philosophy and CV). However, teaching portfolios are infrequently required in the initial application package for academic searches. As with reprints and writing samples, it is best to not submit a teaching portfolio unless it is directly requested. However, if you have compiled an impressive teaching portfolio, you can consider offering it in the interview stage with an institution that highly values teaching. Before submitting a teaching portfolio that has not been requested, you should evaluate whether it will strengthen your application. For example, if a lengthy portfolio is included with a preliminary application, you run the risk of frustrating search committee members with unnecessary documents. Even if it is not a required component of the initial application, it is possible that you will be asked to submit a teaching portfolio at a later point in the screening process. Because it would be challenging to construct a teaching portfolio quickly, it can be useful to have a draft prepared and the information compiled early in the application process so that you could send out the requested portfolio in a timely fashion. In addition, the reflection involved in creating the portfolio should help you prepare for interviews (Rodriguez-Farrar, 2008).

PURPOSE AND COMMON COMPONENTS

Although they can be included in applications for faculty positions, teaching portfolios are typically used for professional development (as a means to reflect on and improve one's teaching) and as an evaluative product for personnel decisions such as tenure, promotion, or teaching awards (Mues & Sorcinelli, 2000). Edgerton, Hutchings, and Quinlan (1991) offered a more extensive description of these two main purposes of a teaching portfolio. First, the process of creating a teaching portfolio is necessarily a developmental process because both selecting and organizing the materials that go into a portfolio requires a consideration of one's teaching practices. Purposeful reflection on what is and is not effective is likely to generate improvements in one's teaching practice. Second, the documentation provided in a teaching portfolio is contextualized evidence of teaching practice and effectiveness that can be evaluated by hiring, personnel, and award committees. In this context, the specific benefit of a teaching portfolio is that it is not exclusively a report of student evaluations. Rather, a portfolio offers a range of evidence from a variety of sources, including sample syllabi, peer or consultant teaching evaluations, sample student work, evidence of successful research supervisions, and faculty development efforts.

FORMATTING AND SAMPLES

The teaching portfolio contains two fundamental components: supporting evidence and reflections on that evidence (Rodriguez-Farrar, 2008). The body of the teaching portfolio includes a five- to eight-page written narrative that highlights, explains, and reflects on evidence of teaching experiences and effectiveness. The purpose of these texts is to organize and interpret the evidence for the reader so that it can be easily referenced and understood. In addition to explaining attached evidence, the body of the portfolio should also include your teaching experience and responsibilities, convey your teaching style, review your teaching philosophy, and include your efforts to improve your teaching. Evidence and data (e.g., sample syllabi, student work, evaluations) are often included in the form of multiple appendices, which usually consist of about eight to 15 or more pages (Rodriguez-Farrar, 2008).

A variety of factors will dictate the format and components of teaching portfolios, including the primary purpose, intended audience, and institutional context (Mues & Sorcinelli, 2000). Although there is significant variability in what can and should be included as supporting evidence, Seldin (1993) emphasized that materials and information in the teaching portfolio should be derived from multiple sources. The premise behind including several sources of information is that they offer multiple perspectives (including those of the instructor, students, and colleagues) that can provide a clearer and perhaps more reliable account of one's teaching activities and effectiveness. Exhibit 4.2 outlines the types of materials that can be included in the portfolio and offers an organizational strategy for presenting supporting evidence. Although it could be tempting to include every piece of supporting material you can obtain, it is vital that you are purposeful in deciding what to include. It is also important to recognize that "supporting evidence" does not necessarily include only successful aspects of your teaching repertoire. "Discussing why a teaching strategy did not work and how you have changed or will change it is evidence that you can adapt and improve as a teacher" (Mues & Sorcinelli, 2000, p. 4). The

EXHIBIT 4.2

Suggested Materials for a Teaching Portfolio

Self-Generated Materials:
- Teaching statement or philosophy.
- List of courses taught, including title of the class, year or term taught, total enrollment, and student demographics (e.g., number of majors, upper or lower division).
- Representative course syllabi from classes you have taught (or an adapted preexisting syllabus if you have not taught your own class).
- Sample course materials (e.g., course assignments, handouts, exams, and other materials used for formative or summative evaluation).
- A description of how your courses, assignments, and teaching techniques have changed in response to student feedback or instructor growth.
- Descriptions of nontraditional teaching activities (e.g., supervision of teaching or laboratory assistants; interaction with students during office hours, email correspondence, and other out of classroom contact with students).
- Descriptions of mentoring activities, goals, and approaches (e.g., work with undergraduate research assistants, honors thesis students, formal or informal graduate student mentees; serving on undergraduate or graduate thesis or dissertation committees).
- A description of advising responsibilities, goals, and approaches (e.g., number of persons you advise, self-generated advising materials, any assistance planning for employment or graduate school you have done).
- Professional development in teaching (e.g., courses you have taken; workshops, conferences, or trainings you have attended on teaching).

Materials from Others
- A summary sheet of student course evaluation data (including title of the class, year/term taught, total enrollment, and average scores/range for each quantitative item).
- A summary of student course evaluation comments (if available). You should provide select quotations that help illustrate various aspects of your teaching philosophy.
- List of teaching awards and certificates.
- Teaching evaluation by faculty member or consultant from you institutions center for teaching and learning.
- Informal student testimonials (e.g., emails or thank you cards received from students).
- Documentation of professional development activities related to teaching.

Products of Good Teaching
- Examples of student work (e.g., final papers, essays from exams, discussion questions, etc.).
- Evidence of successful research supervision (e.g., final theses, conference presentations).
- A summary or table of noteworthy achievements of mentored students (e.g., awards, admissions to graduate school, employment, or other accomplishments).

Potential Supplemental Items
- Descriptions and evaluations of new and innovative courses or projects.
- A videotape of a typical class session.
- A statement by your graduate advisor or the department chair assessing your teaching contributions.
- Contributions to a professional journal on teaching in the discipline.
- Description of service to or membership in professional or university committees on curriculum or teaching issues.
- A summary of participation in off-campus activities related to teaching in the discipline, such as working with local community groups in educational campaigns.
- Evidence of help given to peers and colleagues leading to improvement of their teaching.

Note. Data from Kaplan (1998) and Seldin (1993).

outline provides a possible organizational strategy that can be modified as needed.

Once your supportive evidence has been gathered and organized into appendices, each section of presented material should be summarized in a reflective narrative or in the main body of your portfolio. This textual component allows you to connect and contextualize your experiences within your teaching goals and philosophy. The challenge is to produce cohesive, informative, and thoughtful summaries of the material you have gathered, some of which may not be easily integrated (Rodriguez-Farrar, 2008). To facilitate quick reading by busy search committee members, the writing should be concise and to the point, with the goal of giving contextual clarification about your materials where needed. Each statement should be relatively brief and can be formatted as either a narrative or as bulleted points. Your statements should refer to your evidence but not actually require the reader to refer to specific aspects of each relevant appendix. Instead, "describe your evidence, explain its importance and direct the reader to the appropriate appendices as documentation of your statement" (Rodriguez-Farrar, 2008, p. 10).

One of the common challenges in constructing a teaching portfolio or preparing "evidence of teaching effectiveness" for job applications is integrating and summarizing student evaluations. This component of the teaching portfolio is frequently specifically requested in job applications. Because student evaluations are usually highly variable and do not typically present a unified view of one's teaching, they can often appear inconsistent and therefore be confusing to interpret. The benefit of reviewing, organizing, and analyzing your evaluations is to add insight to the quantitative and qualitative data and to clarify criticisms and praise. For example, if you received particularly negative comments in one class, perhaps it was because of substantial changes in course design that term or because it was the first time you taught that class. One possible method for organizing the presentation of student comments (or other qualitative data) is to group the comments into themes that highlight different aspects of your teaching that you want to emphasize to the search committee. Provide a summary that describes the emergent themes, and then use headers with sample comments to present the data. A visual technique for presenting quantitative evaluation data is to plot numerical data from evaluations of one class over several terms to document trends in student evaluations. By presenting scores on individual items along a time line, less emphasis is placed on any given item, course, or term. Furthermore, if a single data point is particularly low, you may choose to discuss factors in that particular class that could have contributed to the deviation.

When preparing your portfolio, consider working with a mentor (or mentors). This person need not be your research advisor or teaching supervisor; instead, seek assistance and feedback from a faculty member within or outside your department who is interested in promoting high-quality teaching. A consultant from a campus teaching or instructional center would likely be a good resource for this process (Mues & Sorcinelli, 2000).

Supplemental Documents for Professional Applications

Advertisements for the majority of nonacademic positions will simply request a cover letter and résumé with several references. Additional documents are not typically required, though several sometimes are. One of these is the salary history. Although the majority of companies have an established budget for each advertised position, these budgets are frequently flexible, and the resulting salary is often dependent on the candidate's skills and salary history (S. Campbell, 2010). However, when an organization requests a salary history, it may be an indication that the budget may be less flexible and that salary requirements may be, at least initially, an important factor in narrowing down potential candidates. If this information is requested, do not include it in your cover letter or résumé. Create a new document that matches the layout and format of these other documents, and then, following the reverse chronological layout of your résumé or CV, present your entries beginning with your most recent position. The information should be organized as follows: job title, institution or company name, dates of employment, annual salary (or beginning and ending salary to show growth; S. Campbell, 2010). Keep in mind that you should carefully choose how and when to disclose your salary history because you may inadvertently limit your options for salary negotiation. To maintain as much flexibility for negotiating, it is typically recommended that if the job posting does not request salary information, do not offer it.

Some nonacademic institutions, particularly government agencies, require an application form to be filled out before there is any review of your application documents. Oftentimes, the application will to go through a human resources department first, meaning that if you do not spend sufficient time on the application, it may never make it to the individuals who will select the candidate. In addition, in some cases, applications may be scanned by a computer, and if the right words do not appear in the response field, the computer will give the application a low score, and it will not get forwarded to the selection group. Be sure you research what words and information should be included in answer to any open-ended question required for the job you are seeking.

The Bottom Line: Top Recommendations for New Doctorates

Research statements, teaching philosophies, and teaching portfolios act as supplemental documentation of your research and teaching accomplishments and are often required elements of applications for faculty positions. Although there is a lot of variation in what is requested and produced, several conventions exist that can help guide you in the production of each part of your application. Begin developing them early, and seek extensive and ongoing feedback, because these documents can be particularly important in later stages of the hiring process.

RESEARCH STATEMENTS

Your research statement should convince search committees that you have developed a unified program of research that has already made or will soon make significant contributions to your field of study. It should also convince readers that you are well positioned to continue this line of research at their institution. Furthermore, your statement should be tailored to the institution, emphasizing either your ability to involve undergraduates in your research or your ability to procure external funding, depending on which would likely be more important to the search committee.

TEACHING STATEMENTS

In addition to conveying your commitment to teaching, the teaching statement should clearly and concisely present your teaching values, goals, pedagogy, methods of assessment, and efforts at professional development and improvement. Although the concepts you present will likely be abstract, it is important to ground these ideas with examples from your own teaching experiences or with techniques and activities you plan on incorporating into future classes you could teach. This statement should be modified according to the types of institutions to which you are applying; for example, a teaching statement for a liberal arts college will look different to one for a school with primarily large class sizes.

TEACHING PORTFOLIOS

Although teaching portfolios are not frequently required components of initial application dossiers, elements of teaching portfolios can be requested early in the application process, and complete portfolios may be requested during the interview stage. Thus, it can be useful to compile the materials typically found in teaching portfolios and draft a reflective statement to accompany the supporting evidence. This can be helpful in preparing a portfolio to submit later and in facilitating your thoughtful reflection on your teaching practices in preparation for entering the job market and ultimately taking a position as an instructional faculty member.

Securing Strong Letters of Recommendation

5

> Your CV tells what you did. Your letters of recommendation tell how well you did it.
>
> —*R. M. Reis, "Getting Great Letters of Recommendation"*

The majority of your application package (cover letter, curriculum vitae [CV] or résumé, and, often, supplemental documents such as research and teaching statements) contains information written by you. Letters of recommendation or references, however, are usually the hiring committee's only opportunity to gain information about you as a candidate from other individuals. Typically, the individuals supporting your candidacy know you well, have worked closely with you, and are also authorities in your field, making them well positioned to assess your work (University of California, Berkeley, Career Center, 2009). Indeed, your references frequently provide hiring committees with the first independent assessments of your capabilities and potential. Although search committee members place varying degrees of importance on letters of recommendation when first reviewing applications, it is likely that your references will be examined closely after the initial screening of the applicant pool (University of California, Berkeley, Career Center, 2009). Research on procedures search committees use to hire new faculty revealed that letters of recommendation were in the top three criteria used to assess applicants (Sheehan, McDevitt, & Ross, 1998), and Reis (2001) suggested that advancement in the selection process will most likely occur only if you have included positive letters of recommendation.

Through your experiences in graduate school, you have likely learned how to select appropriate people to list as references or to write letters of recommendation for you. Many of the same considerations apply when selecting references to include in your applications for advanced professional positions, but there are a few other special considerations and logistics to bear in mind as well.

Building Professional Relationships

Because having first-rate references is important, it is best to begin cultivating personal relationships with potential letter writers early in your graduate career. It is typical for potential employers to check or request letters from three references for each candidate, though occasionally some will ask for up to five. Thus, be prepared to find anywhere from three to five people who can write knowledgeably about your skills and experiences. Some candidates have one extra letter at the ready for every application in anticipation of some getting lost or misfiled or because letter writers are not always reliable and may not submit their letter before the deadline. If all letters do arrive on time, it is possible that including an extra letter could strengthen your application (although it could backfire in some cases as well). However, remember that "it's better to have three very strong letters than to have four letters, only three of which are very strong" (Ernst, 2002, para. 2). Furthermore, the quality of the letters notwithstanding, including materials that were not specifically requested (e.g., letters when only references were requested or four references when only three were requested) may be perceived as an inability to follow directions or an unwillingness to customize your application to that particular institution. Sending a short e-mail to the search committee chair could help you ascertain whether supplemental letters will be regarded positively or negatively.

There are several ways that you can build these important relationships. First, take time to socialize with faculty at laboratory or department functions and take opportunities to informally discuss your career interests and goals with faculty members. Think about asking whether you can attend the research meetings of other faculty members so that you can become acquainted with them on an ongoing basis.

> Don't be afraid to ask senior scientists for advice about various career possibilities. The vast majority will welcome the opportunity to chat (after all, they were once asking for the same guidance) and in the process will come to know you in a more well-rounded way. (Reis, 2001, p. 2)

If you find yourself preparing to go on the job market without these relationships already in place, try to start catching up as soon as possible by setting up individual meetings and attending as many formal and informal meetings as possible with potential letter writers. Although you may not have a "history" with them, they will likely recognize your initiative and get to know your current work.

Casting a broad net to establish positive relationships with faculty members is important because any faculty member can act as an informal reference, either by your choosing or without your knowledge. Although the legal guidelines for checking references are complex, many employers have policies in place that allow them to check with any former supervisor, whether or not they are listed as a reference and with or without your permission. However, it is common for potential employers to inform you if they will be contacting individuals not listed as references. It is also possible that someone at one or more of the institutions to which you are applying happens to know a faculty member in your department. In this case, it is quite common for them to informally contact that person to get the "inside scoop" on you. If the faculty member has positive things to say about you, it can be immeasurably helpful for your candidacy (and, conversely, negative comments can derail your candidacy). It is sometimes hard to predict which of your networked connections will substantially assist your job search efforts.

Selecting Letter Writers

In general, it is important not to omit obvious people such as past supervisors and advisors from your list of references. When choosing who will write your letters, it is important that your primary academic or dissertation advisor should write one of them (Reis, 2001). If you are in a postdoctoral position, your supervisor should also write a letter. If a prior advisor or supervisor is omitted from a list of references, the typical conclusion from hiring committees is that you have a poor relationship with him or her and that he or she would have written you a negative recommendation (Ernst, 2002). Occasionally, graduate or postdoctoral students find themselves facing the dilemma of not being able to secure a strong letter (or any letter) from their advisor. If you encounter this issue, your best course of action may be to approach the department chair, most senior faculty member in your department, or another tenured faculty member that you trust for advice (University of California, Berkeley, Career Center, 2009)—perhaps a faculty member in whose class you did well. It is possible that this individual will agree to serve as a reference for you and may even be able to address the situation with your advisor directly or indirectly (Reis, 2001). Be aware that the hiring institution may decide, especially in the final stages of the selection process, to contact your supervisor or advisor even if she or he is not listed in your references.

The other two to three letter writers should be faculty members or supervisors who are familiar with your abilities that are relevant to type of job you are seeking. Thus, if you are applying for an academic position, you should have at least one letter writer who can write about your research abilities and another who can write about your teaching abilities (Mangum, 2009). Although there may be some benefit to having the most well-known or respected member of your graduate faculty write you a letter, it is generally considered more important to select letter writers with whom you have had long-term working relationships, even if they are junior faculty members (Reis, 2001); a vague recommendation letter from a well-known professor may do more harm than good. The personal knowledge of your professional skills and abilities that is gained through a long-term working relationship will enable the letter writer to substantiate his or her general observations of your abilities with specific examples or stories about your successes. Furthermore, because the current convention is for long and detailed letters (i.e., one to two pages), the most effective ones will convey an in-depth understanding of your work and include a basis or rationale for the writer's endorsement of your candidacy (Ernst, 2002). Of course, the writer should have a positive opinion of you and your abilities and should not have a conflict of interest (e.g., being the advisor of another applicant for the same position).

For academic positions and research-oriented professional positions, it is important that at least one letter writer or reference be able to talk about your research expertise. Vick and Furlong (2008) explained that letters addressing candidates' research should contextualize the research and convey the importance and impact of the work. It can also be helpful if the letter speaks to the promise of your continued professional development and growth as well as your abilities to supervise or direct others (Reis, 2001).

From the Trenches—Employer Experiences and Advice

If a candidate wants to teach at a liberal arts institution, then he or she should seek out teaching experience at such an institution and seek feedback and critique from someone at that institution. I've done this for several grad students at a research university in town and it has helped them on the job market. We do not give a lot of weight to recommendation letters from research supervisors that talk about the teaching abilities of candidates. In general, we're pretty sure the writer is probably not highly knowledgeable about teaching and has probably not closely supervised the teaching of the candidate.

—Stephen C., PhD in experimental psychology, professor at Samford University

At least one of your letter writers or references should also be able to speak about your abilities and potential as a teacher, even if you are applying for positions only at research-oriented institutions. It is common for teaching-oriented institutions to stipulate that at least one of your letters come from someone who is familiar with your teaching. This letter writer should able to address your interest in, experience with, and effectiveness in teaching and working with students. It would be beneficial if he or she has observed you leading a class and can speak about your style as a lecturer or your manner of interacting with research assistants. If this person has supervised you as a teaching assistant, he or she could speak about students' reactions to your teaching and about your overall responsibilities and experience. If your letter writers have never seen you teach, it could be useful to ask them whether they would be willing to sit in on a section, class, or research meeting you are leading or whether you could present a guest lecture in their class. Your letter writers should be able to speak about your teaching abilities on the basis of direct experience; however, if you are not in the position to have potential letter writers observe your teaching, you can offer them your teaching evaluations and other evidence of teaching effectiveness you have assembled for your application. You could also ask whether you could give a formal or informal research talk at your institution—at a departmental colloquium or graduate research conference, for example—and invite your letter writers to attend (University of California, Berkeley, Career Center, 2009).

Finally, it is important that your letter writers are generally knowledgeable about the places to which you are applying and about the norms of letter writing in your discipline. If your letter writer is familiar with the specific institutions or organizations to which you are applying, they will be better positioned to emphasize your strengths and qualifications that are suited to the position. Furthermore, a letter that fits the conventions of letter writing in your discipline will increase the likelihood that the letter is taken seriously. Ernst (2002) also reminded candidates that

> people most similar to the letter readers will be able to write most persuasively: that is, for an academic or research job, focus on academics and researchers as references, and for a corporate job, your industrial bosses may will be best (para. 2).

Figure 5.1 shows an example of a letter written in support of a job application. (Note that the names have been changed from the original letter.)

Once you have decided who your three to five letter writers will be, you should set up appointments to formally ask them to write your letters of recommendation. Typically, you should ask them during the spring term (May or June) to write your letters for the following fall or winter.

FIGURE 5.1

March 28, 2003

Dr. Donald Werner
Department of Psychology
Lynchburg College
1501 Lakeside Drive
Lynchburg, VA 24501

Dear Dr. Werner,

I have been asked by Dr. Efren Soto for a letter of recommendation in support of his application for the faculty position available in your department. It is my pleasure to provide this letter and my support for Efren and his application.

Efren is an outstanding teacher and researcher, and he has been quite generous in his service to the university, the community, and to the profession. You will find that this letter will end with my highest recommendation and without reservation—he's that good. I have come to this conclusion after knowing Efren for about 3 years, the last 2 years as a faculty member. Thus, I feel that I know him quite well.

Efren is one of the most dedicated teachers that I know, period. Given that I am a Fellow of Division 2 of APA, I know quite a few outstanding teachers. Efren sees his teaching as a process of continuous improvement. I think that he takes every last ounce of feedback from teaching a class and strives for significant improvement the next time he teaches. For instance, Efren recently started teaching our Research Methods course, a rigorous course and the only 4-credit course in our department. I had previously taught the course for about 4 years. Efren skillfully kept the components of the course that fit with the teaching style and goals, and added wonderfully innovative ideas. Early in the semester he had students working together in groups, operationalizing research ideas and struggling with how to define the measurement process. After he told me about this project, I started thinking to myself, "Why didn't I do that when I taught the course?" He's using the classroom jigsaw technique this semester in another class that he is teaching. What I like about Efren is that he is willing to take risks in the classroom—try something new and see if it works or not. This approach pays off handsomely for him, not only in teaching improvement, but also in that teaching-related issues has become one of his lines of research. His presentations at conferences often center on teaching ideas and his systematic assessment of the relative success of those teaching approaches.

Efren's energy and enthusiasm for teaching appear boundless. I wish I had worked that hard on the craft of teaching when I was at the stage of my career that he is at. His ideas are refreshing and innovative; he makes me re-examine my own teaching strategies. For

Sample letter of recommendation. Note that the names have been changed from the original letter.

FIGURE 5.1 (*Continued*)

Letter of Recommendation for Dr. Efren Soto
March 28, 2003
Page 2

instance, he has General Psychology work in groups to design observational studies, has Physiological Psychology students role-play unusual behavioral problems, has Cognitive Psychology students design advertising campaigns based on psychological principles, has Research Methods students doing innovative group projects, and has Statistical Methods students interact more deeply with the material—what wonderful ideas! Not only do these examples point out his refreshing approach, but they also address Efren's versatility as an instructor. He has been a great "utility infielder," able to adeptly teach a wide variety of courses.

One of the things I like best about Efren is that he has been able to find that balance between teaching and research. They are truly symbiotic activities. For instance, Efren is actively presenting and publishing work in the teaching of psychology field, but he also studies other areas. He understands the balance between the two activities, and values both. What is refreshing about his approach is that he successfully intertwines the two. Thus, he can be innovative in the classroom, yet take a scientific approach in evaluating the effectiveness of the teaching technique. Then, in true Efren style, he is generous with his talents, sharing these techniques not only with his colleagues locally but also with colleagues at regional conferences such as Midwestern Psychological Association meetings.

What about Efren's work with students? In a word—amazing. For instance, this semester he has 12 (!) research assistants working on a myriad of projects. I have to admit that the semester before, he was a bit of a slacker, working with only 11 students! Efren clearly goes beyond the minimums set by the department and excels at his job. Why? He is intrinsically motivated; he has research ideas and he wants to pursue them. He gives our best and brightest undergraduate students a chance to shine and an opportunity to grow in working with him as a research assistant. I have watched this process first-hand, and he has turned into a first-rate mentor for our students. This loss of talent in this area alone will be devastating for our department, but another department will reap the benefits. As evidence of this dedication to teaching, just examine Efren's CV and look at the pervasiveness of student co-authors on conference presentations and publications!

Let me address Efren's performance from the perspective of a colleague. This year I served as committee chair of our departmental Personnel Committee. We evaluate each of the tenure-track faculty members. I received Efren's permission to discuss his evaluation results in this letter. We evaluate in the areas of teaching, research, and service, and we use a three-tiered system: does not meet expectations, meets expectations, and exceeds expectations. Even though the system is fuzzy at times, Efren had an outstanding year in 2002. Efren exceeded expectations in all categories: teaching, research, and service (I have to say this is unusual for someone this early in their career).

Phone: (208) 426-1993   Fax: (208) 426-4386   Email: elandru@boisestate.edu

Sample letter of recommendation.

FIGURE 5.1 (*Continued*)

Letter of Recommendation for Dr. Efren Soto
March 28, 2003
Page 3

Efren's not leaving this institution because he can't handle it—on the contrary, he's looking to leave because he values what he does, he's good at it, and he's looking for a place that is a better match. You have no idea how much I respect him for that, even though it will be hard to lose him, both professionally and personally. Let me say that Efren is both a valued colleague and a friend. You will find him quite personable and a pleasure to work with. He brings an energy and an intellect to the workplace that is unparalleled. In fact, I would say he is the total and complete package if only his racquetball serve were better. I guess everyone needs at least one area for improvement.

As you can imagine, **I recommend Dr. Efren Soto to you with my absolutely highest recommendation and without reservation**. He will be an amazing addition to your faculty. Clearly, our loss is your gain. If I can be of any additional help, please contact me directly.

Sincerely,

R. Eric Landrum, PhD
Professor
Department of Psychology

Phone: (208) 426-1993   Fax: (208) 426-4386   Email: elandru@boisestate.edu

Sample letter of recommendation.

Although you may feel comfortable asking them in an e-mail to provide you with a letter, asking them in person is more formal and respectful. Remember that you should not feel that you are imposing when you ask for letters of recommendation. If you have a good working relationship with your mentors, they recognize that you will be eventually asking for letters of support, and they understand that it is part of their professional responsibility. However, you should approach your potential letter writers with respect rather than expectation (Ernst, 2002).

If you are unsure whether prospective letter writers have enough experience with you or have a positive enough impression of you to provide a strong letter, you should ask them. "After all, if you're going to compete with people who have uniformly glowing letters of recommendation, a mildly positive letter from someone who doesn't really know you can actually do more harm than good" (Social Psychology Network, 2011, para. 3). Ascertaining whether a potential reference can offer you a positive recommendation can be awkward; the University of California, Berkeley, Career Center (2009) suggested that you ask faculty members whether they believe "that they know you and your work well enough to write an effective letter" (para. 16). Approaching your letter writers this way not only provides them with an easy way to decline but also assures you that those who agree will write a positive letter. (See Exhibit 5.1 for the effects of inflated vs. noninflated letters of recommendation.) It is especially important to assess ahead of time whether you will receive a positive letter, because it is standard practice for candidates to waive the right to view any letters of recommendation, and it is thus likely you will never have the opportunity to review what the letter writer wrote about you.

Following your initial request, and at least a month or two in advance of the need for your letters, you should make appointments to speak with everyone you expect to write a letter for you. These meetings will give you the opportunity to discuss the types of position you hope to obtain and to get thoughtful feedback about factors you should consider in your application. You should also use the meetings as opportunities to remind your letter writers about your relationship with them, with the goal of emphasizing the ways in which your letter writer could provide the best support for your application.

From the Trenches—Employer Experiences and Advice

Make sure your recommenders understand the job you are applying for, and can talk about your strengths related to that job, not some other job.

—Anonymous

EXHIBIT 5.1

What the Literature Says . . . About Inflated and Noninflated Letters of Recommendation

Nicklin and Roch (2008) conducted an experiment that examined the effect of letters of recommendation that were either "inflated" or "noninflated." A pilot test revealed that inflated letters were rated as more inflated, less useful, less balanced, and less honest that noninflated letters, suggesting that inflation in letters of recommendation is relatively easy to detect. However, when undergraduate students reviewed these letters, applicants with inflated letters or recommendations were perceived more positively than applicants with noninflated letters. Furthermore, participants indicated that they were more likely to hire applicants with an inflated letter and rated them as more likely to be successful in the company than applicants with noninflated letters. It is interesting that participants who received an inflated letter reported it to be less honest and more exaggerated than did participants who received a noninflated letter. Overall, these results imply that even though individuals may be able to recognize an exaggerated letter, they are still significantly positively influenced by the inflated contents of the recommendation letters.

You should discuss the important aspects of your relationship with each letter writer because it will improve your application if you ask each individual to write about specific aspects of your work. It is extremely important for your collection of letters to provide detailed information about how you meet the central skills and experience requirements that search committees are seeking in their applicants. It is especially important for female applicants to offer information to their letter writers that emphasizes the agentic nature of their skills, because research has found that letters of recommendation for women tend to focus on communal skills, which are evaluated less positively by employers (Madera, Hebl, & Martin, 2009). Thus, for an academic position, your letters must explain the importance of your research as well as outline the qualities that will make you an effective teacher and good colleague (Reis, 2001). However, even though you have likely selected one faculty member who can speak about a specific skill (e.g., your teaching ability), that person will not know you expect her or him to address or focus on this skill unless you specifically mention it. So, for example, when you approach the letter writer who you want to write about your teaching abilities, you should not only provide him or her with documents and information supporting your teaching effectiveness (see the next section) but also explicitly ask him or her to mention your teaching skills (University of California, Berkeley, Career Center, 2009). Even though these conversations are important for ensuring that your skills are adequately described in your letters, remember to approach these requests carefully because some faculty may perceive them as demanding if they are not made respectfully.

If you are in graduate school, it can be particularly useful to talk with your advisor or dissertation chair before approaching your letter writers. He or she can help you decide who might best speak about your different skills and may even help you talk to other letter writers about what to emphasize. Furthermore, if you are still working on finishing your dissertation, it will be necessary for your advisor to specifically address the state of your dissertation (e.g., what is currently completed and when it will be finished). Your advisor should also be the one to address any aspect of your application package that might be out of the ordinary. For example, if you have taken an unusually long time to complete your degree because of your desire to enhance the quality of your scholarship or pursue a research project that required access to a hard-to-find population, your advisor should be the one to explain the delay (University of California, Berkeley, Career Center, 2009).

Materials to Provide to Letter Writers

In addition to having a conversation with your letter writers about your career goals and possible topics to emphasize in their letters, you should provide each reference with a package of information that not only outlines the positions you are applying for but also includes specific material that will help them compose a letter that demonstrates their confidence in you and your abilities. Ideally, this package should include evidence of accomplishments not otherwise available in your application materials. For example, provide basic details that they can use in the letter, such as when you entered your program, when you took their class (and what grade you received), when you worked with them and in what capacity, and ongoing or upcoming associations you have or will have with them. It is also useful to provide them with a bulleted document that includes precise descriptions of your work, with specific examples of positive interactions you have had with them. This might include being nominated by them for an award or scholarship, being hired by them for a selective research assistant or teaching assistant position, or being given positive feedback by them on a presentation or paper. It can also be useful to remind them of information about your service activities, such as reviewing articles, providing service to professional organizations, or even providing departmental and community service (Vick & Furlong, 2008). Last, you can supplement your package with the latest copy of your CV or résumé, research and teaching statements, recent research papers, teaching evaluations, and sample syllabi. (See Exhibit 5.2 for a checklist of materials to provide to letter writers.)

EXHIBIT 5.2

Checklist of Materials to Provide to Letter Writers

▪ List of positions for which you are applying, with contact names and addresses, due dates, basic information about the position, and how to submit the letter (i.e., mail, e-mail, online submission)
▪ Descriptions of your noteworthy interactions with the letter writer
▪ Curriculum vitae and sample cover letter
▪ Research statement and reprints, preprints, or other writing samples
▪ Teaching statement, teaching evaluation summary, and sample syllabi or assignment prompts

---

It is particularly important that you provide your letter writers with information about the types of positions you are applying for and where. This information is important not only for logistical purposes but also so that your letter writers can modify their letters to fit each type of position and organization. For example, if you are applying to both teaching-oriented and research-oriented academic institutions, your letter writers may want to write a separate letter for each or equally emphasize your teaching and research abilities in one letter. If you are also applying for clinical positions, a unique set of letters should likely be used for these applications (Huang-Pollock & Mikami, 2007). For example, when applying for a clinical position, your letter writer should write specifically and in detail about your clinical abilities and skills related to interpersonal practice, whereas for an academic position it will be much more important for the letter writer to focus on your teaching and research skills. If your letter writer offers or prefers to write separate letters for each of your applications, be sure to ask whether you can help by providing specific information about each position.

Be sure to check whether the faculty member or the administrative assistant who is preparing the letter has a preferred format. You should provide a list of all positions to which you are applying, including the organization or institution name and address and the position name and number. Although some people prefer receiving separate requests for letters, letters are usually sent out in batches on the due dates, so it is helpful to provide as complete a list as possible at the outset. However, because some advertisements are posted the week the applications are due, you should ask your letter writers in advance how they would prefer to deal with those last-minute postings. If they have already agreed to complete additional letters with short notice, you will feel more comfortable asking for those letters, despite the short notice. Advance organization and preparation makes you appear

---

From the Trenches—Applicant Experiences and Advice

Most schools have their own letter of recommendation services you can use. However, I personally found that using Interfolio was helpful. It's a credentialing service that is reasonably priced and allowed me to apply to jobs on my own time table without continually bothering my letter writers. They got an invitation to upload a letter from the site, did so, and then I could have the service send out letters (via web form, email or snail mail) whenever I wanted. Especially because I am on internship in another state than my letter writers, *the service* gave me peace of mind to know that the letters would arrive on time, in packets with my other materials, and I didn't have to bug my advisor or other letter writers. The only possible downside I saw to this service was that the letters weren't individually addressed to each school, but this didn't seem to harm me in any way. Still, you may want to consider that if you plan to use such a service.

—Jennifer V., PhD in psychology

---

more serious and professional in addition to easing the task for your letter writer.

What Will They Write About?

Range et al. (1991) reported the common components of letters of recommendation after a review of 150 letters written for internship applicants. They described the typical letter as starting with the applicant's name and desired position. Next, writers typically described their association with the applicant and how long or how well they had known each other. The letter then usually described the applicant's academic, assessment, therapy and/or research skills, followed by an overview of the applicant's behavior in supervision, additional accomplishments, personality characteristics, or interpersonal skills. In closing statements, the typical letter writer suggested that the applicant would be successful in the position and offered a recommendation without reservations. Although letters written for exclusively academic positions will probably emphasize slightly different skills, the format of your letters will likely be similar. Given that this is the typical format that your letter writers will use, it can be helpful to provide them with specific details they can use to fill out these sections, such as the history of your relationship with them and reminders of particularly positive past interactions you have had with them. As Schall (2006) said: "A letter of recommendation lives or dies on its examples and evidence" (para. 7).

Sometimes letter writers will ask you to write your own letter for them to modify and sign.

> You should do so if requested, but this is not such a good idea in general. First, it indicates that the letter writer is not enthusiastic enough about your application to write his or her own letter. Second, you may not know the hidden language of letters of reference, so you may inadvertently err by commission or omission. Third, the letter won't sound like the person's other letters. Fourth, the letter won't add much to your own statement, and this homogeneity will make your application less compelling: it's better for the evaluators to have multiple perspectives on your personality and accomplishments. (Ernst, 2002, para. 9)

Following Up

One of the most frustrating parts of securing reference letters for job applications is that it can be hard to know whether they were sent or received, because letters are typically sent separately from the application package. Brems, Lampman, and Johnson (1995) reported that just over half of all applications reviewed for their study included a complete set of letters, with 20% of applicants not providing any. Although it is likely that some applicants failed to obtain the correct number of letter writers, it is also possible that the letters got lost in transit or by the receiving institutions or that the letter writers forgot to write them or did not send them on time. Because there is no drawback to having your letters arrive before the rest of your application package, it can help to request that letters be sent out early, though this is not always feasible. It can be helpful to check a few days before the deadline whether your application materials have arrived and whether they are complete. If you are missing one or more letters, you can politely request that your letter writer resend them.

Finally, it is important that you write a formal thank-you note to each of your letter writers. This can be done once all of the letters are completed or when the bulk of the letters have been sent out. It can also be useful to update your letter writers as you receive positive feedback about your application, such as invitations for interviews, partly because those invitations may result in the hiring committee contacting your letter writer for an updated reference. It is polite to let each letter writer know if you accept a job; most letter writers will be happy to hear that their efforts helped you secure a desirable position. Furthermore, you should plan on keeping in contact with your letter writers over the long term, not only because you may ask them for future letters of recommendation when you change positions but also because they will be your professional colleagues.

Special Considerations for Professional Positions

The largest difference between references for academic and professional positions is that advertisements for professional positions are much less likely to ask for letters of recommendation to be included with the application and will more likely ask you to provide a list of references instead. If you become a finalist for the position, members of the hiring committee are most likely to call and ask to speak with your reference. By phoning references, potential employers can get candid recommendations, because the reference person must provide quick and unrehearsed answers to questions about your competencies. This can be a much different experience to writing a letter for the individual providing your reference; thus, it is important that you prepare your academic letter writers for this possibility if you are applying for professional positions.

Your task as a job seeker is to provide your references with information to help prepare them to be the best reference possible. Make sure you give them a few points to which they can refer when they receive a call from the potential employer. In addition, make sure that they have the most up-to-date copy of your CV or résumé available. Besides giving them the names of the companies and positions to which you are applying, also give them some indication of why you think you are a good fit for each position. As is recommended for academic references, you should also provide several examples of experiences they have had with you that exemplify your skills and strengths. Help them speak about the skills you demonstrate in an academic context in nonacademic terms, such as by describing your leadership and management abilities. Keep in mind that telephone reference checks will typically involve asking about both strengths and weaknesses in leadership, management, presentation abilities, and communication. Furthermore, in selecting your references for your applications for professional positions, remember that people most similar to the people on the hiring committee will be able to provide the more persuasive recommendation. Thus, for a corporate job, any supervisors in the industrial and organizational area should be on your list of contacts (Ernst, 2002). Overall, there are not many differences between selecting and preparing references for either academic or nonacademic positions. Both require forethought, cultivation of relationships, and preparation.

The Bottom Line:
Top Recommendations for
New Doctorates

Building and maintaining relationships with potential future letters writers whom know you well and with whom you have positive relationships is the first step in preparing for this aspect of your application. Keep records of positive interactions you have with faculty members, including comments on your classwork or e-mail correspondence following a presentation. Once you have selected (and confirmed) who will provide your references, you should provide each letter writer with enough information about the positions, your work, and what they could emphasize in your letter that would best round out your application. Keep in mind that you want your letter writers to specifically speak to those skills and abilities that will be used to evaluate your strengths as a candidate.

The Screening Interviews
Preparing for Success 6

Even though being asked to participate in a screening interview opens up a whole new set of questions and anxiety for most candidates, making it through the first round of screening speaks positively about your potential and preparation. R. W. Campbell, Horner-Devine, Lartigue, and Rollwagen-Bollens (2001) reminded candidates that "being asked to interview for an academic position is a major statement about how the search committee feels about your preparation and potential as a member of their faculty" (p. 4). In addition to seeing the invitation for an interview as an indication of your outstanding application, is also important to keep in mind that the purpose of the off-site "screening" interview is both for the institution or organization to find out whether you would be a good fit for them, as well as for you to find out whether the position and your potential future colleagues are a good fit for you. Indeed, during a phone interview, committee members are not only assessing your ability to substantiate the skills and expertise you outlined in your application materials but also the extent of your interest in the position (Sowers-Hoag & Harrison, 1998).

Off-site screening interviews are common because they provide an intermediary step that can help search committees make the difficult decision of who to invite for on-site or campus interviews. Job searches are expensive and time consuming, so beginning with an off-site phone, video, or conference/convention interview is often the best way for a search committee to further narrow their applicant pool.

These interviews can occur in a number of settings, depending on the discipline and type of job. For many academic positions, one or more members of a search committee will conduct telephone interviews with six to 10 applicants, followed by two to three invitations for a campus visit or on-site interview. For some positions, including professional positions, a campus or on-site visit invitation may be issued without a prior off-site screening interview (Career Advising and Planning Services, 2010). As you begin your job application process, it is important to gather as much information as possible from your advisors, your peers, recent alumni, and other mentors about typical interviewing procedures in your particular specialty area within psychology and for the types of jobs you are seeking.

Goals of the Screening Interview

In a screening interview, your overall goal is to convey an image of yourself as a colleague who will be successful as well as enjoyable to worth with. Therefore, it is important to communicate that you are beginning the transition from graduate school (or postdoctoral position) to professional or academic life (Johnson, 2004). In particular, when relaying your experiences during graduate school or your postdoc training to the interviewers, it is helpful to think about these experiences in terms of accomplishments, not responsibilities. For example, rather than talking about what programs you had to develop and how many clients you had to meet with at your clinical internship, instead describe the programs you were able to successfully develop and the diverse number and type of clients you had the opportunity to work with. The difference between "I have to teach a class" and "I get to teach a class" is subtle but important. Also, thinking about the interview as a conversation taking place between colleagues rather than as reminiscent of your oral qualifying exam will help you emphasize your strengths, appear more interested, and be more collegial (Career Advising and Planning Services, 2010). Last, set a goal of learning something new from the interview. Not only would this provide you with more information about the position and organization but it would also make you appear genuinely interested in what it is like to work at the institution, a quality that would be viewed positively by interviewers (Seelig, 2010).

Overall, the interviewers are looking for signs that you understand what success in the position for which you are applying entails. In academic positions, this would include being a productive scholar, an excellent teacher, and a good citizen in the department and university (Career Advising and Planning Services, 2010). In professional positions, the criteria for success will depend on the position but likely involve timely completion of quality projects as well as excellent leadership, managerial, and communication skills. A job candidate who spends too much time referring to awards they have received and mentioning the names of well-known researchers with whom they have worked may not best exemplify these qualities. The goal, then, is to present yourself as a competent candidate who is willing to learn and adapt to the institution or organization at which you are interviewing. In terms of the volleyball-serve analogy, you should be competent enough to serve the ball over the net but not so aggressive as to hit it out of bounds.

Although finding a colleague with excellence in research and teaching is clearly central in any academic job search, research suggests that "fit with department" is the most important criterion in applicant selection (Burns & Kinkade, 2008; Landrum & Clump, 2004). Expressing genuine excitement and enthusiasm for your work and for the institution to which you are applying will benefit your standing (Johnson, 2004):

> A special challenge with phone interviews is that you have only your voice to use to convey your collegiality. To help your voice do that work by itself, sit upright, smile, lean forward, and even gesture as you talk into the phone, just as you would in person. You may feel a bit odd, but that activity will energize your voice and make it expressive. (para. 27)

Considerations of fit and collegiality are similarly important in professional positions (Wagner, 2000), as discussed in depth in the section on off-site interviews for professional positions. See Exhibit 6.1 for a further discussion of fit as a variable in faculty hiring decisions.

From the Trenches—Employer Experiences and Advice

Do your homework and get to know the institution. Keep in mind that you are evaluating your fit with the department as they are evaluating you—candidates who are gauging fit tend to listen more closely and therefore are perceived as more polite and interested in the department and position.

—PhD in psychology, associate professor in the Southwest

EXHIBIT 6.1

What the Literature Says . . . About Intuition in Faculty Hiring Decisions

It is commonly accepted that there is extensive use of intuition in faculty hiring decisions. Using prior research examining executive assessments in business—a similar hiring process that seeks to fill an individual position from a pool of highly qualified candidates—Mullins and Rogers (2008) explained why intuition tends to be a particularly central evaluative method during interviews. Preliminary screenings of job applications use "quantifiable" measures of job preparedness and future potential success, which typically include a review of publications and teaching experience. Narrowing the pool to include only those with a reasonable expectation of success in the position results in a "restricted range of both cognitive ability and job knowledge" (p. 370), which leads hiring committees to turn their attention to issues of fit. Mullins and Rogers suggested that during the interview stage, using intuitive personal assessments of fit is common both because fit is seen to be independent of more reliable forms of assessment (e.g., number of publications) and because committee members believe (either accurately or erroneously) that the preliminary screenings of more quantifiable information about the candidate minimizes the likelihood of mistakes in hiring decisions made on the basis of intuition.

Preparing for Academic Interviews

The first step in preparing for an academic job interview is to do preliminary research on the institution and, if possible, on the people who will be interviewing you. Search committee members have indicated that what sets the best candidates apart from the rest is their knowledge of the institution and the department (Montell, 2001). At the very least, you need to know whether the institution is a large research university that may be most concerned about your ability to procure external funding, a selective liberal arts college that values good teaching and involving undergraduates in your research, or a midsize institution with a heavy teaching load in addition to research requirements. Doing even a small amount of research on the institution before your interview will allow you to emphasize those of your experiences that correspond to the needs of the institution and will also convey your interest in the position (Johnson, 2004).

It is just as important to review the job description carefully. It can be helpful to print it out or have it accessible electronically during your interview (Montell, 2001). Because search committees prioritize match or fit with the department, making sure you address the needs outlined in the advertisement is imperative. Use the position announcement to help anticipate the department's or organization's needs as best you can, so that when you talk to them you emphasize experiences and quali-

From the Trenches—Applicant Experiences and Advice

I created 5 or 6 Post-it notes of my key talking points for phone interviews (courses I could teach, research plans for 1, 3, and 5 years, ways to involved undergraduates, position on diversity, etc.), as well as a couple of questions that I had for them. Having those points in front of me kept me focused, calm, and limited the amount of stalling that I did while trying to come up with something to say. The creation of these bullet points was also a beneficial exercise.

—Sarah B., PhD in psychology, selective liberal arts college in the Midwest

fications that match what they are seeking in a candidate. It can also help to find out whether anyone in your network has information on the needs of the institution, because job advertisements are not always clearly written and often do not contain enough specific information.

Further investigation into the institution, department, and individual faculty members is also important. You should learn as much as you can, for example, about the student population, the mission of the university, the department's course offerings, the research-to-teaching workload ratio, the background of departmental faculty members, and any other relevant information you can obtain. In particular, be familiar with the names of the classes offered by the department (especially those listed in the advertisement) and be prepared to specifically discuss how you could contribute to any one of the department's ongoing programs or initiatives (Sies, 1996). Institutional and department information for the majority of colleges and universities is easily accessible online. Other sources of background information include college guides, student and university newspapers (often online), faculty members at your current institution, and anyone you know who attended the institution to which you are applying. College and university course catalogs are also excellent sources of information on the goals and characteristics of institutions and of departments within them; these, too, are often available online (Career Advising and Planning Services, 2010).

Before even receiving your first invitation for an interview, you should schedule a practice interview with faculty members and fellow doctoral students. It can be particularly helpful to have some people there who are not especially familiar with your work. It may also be helpful to invite any graduate students who have already participated in a preliminary interview. You can request feedback from your audience about whether you seemed engaged or interested in the position, your level of confidence and professionalism, and whether you appeared to be someone they would want to work with (Heiberger & Vick, 1999).

From the Trenches—Applicant Experiences and Advice

There were some questions I had to completely blunder through a couple of times before I was able to answer them coherently. I cannot emphasize enough how important it is to share questions you were asked in interviews with your colleagues and practice answering the questions with each other.

—PhD in developmental psychology,
assistant professor at a public university in the South

Many screening interviews will be set up with short notice through phone calls (although some departments will e-mail you). Thus, make sure that you are willing and able to accept phone calls at the number you provided on your curriculum vitae. If you do not want to be called at home or on your cell phone, provide a campus or work phone number. Record a brief and professional message on your answering machine or voicemail service (including your first and last name), and check your voicemail and e-mail daily. It is important to return any calls as quickly as possible or risk seeming disinterested in the position. When you receive a call or e-mail inviting you to participate in a screening interview, you should be prepared to gather detailed information about the nature (e.g., telephone or video conferencing) and length of the interview and at least a general idea of who will be interviewing you. If this information is not offered, you should ask for it. It is helpful to keep a pen and paper by the phone along with your calendar and a list of questions you want to ask your contact when you are offered an interview. Because some departments do not call candidates until 2 or 3 days before the actual phone interview, the invitation phone call is often your only chance to collect the information you need to prepare for the interview.

Some interviewers may call and ask to conduct the interview immediately. It is perfectly acceptable for you to decline an interview with such short notice. The best way to deal with an immediate request for an interview is to indicate that you are not available to talk at that moment but are excited to speak with the interviewer soon. One approach is to use a polite excuse such as a meeting, a class, or a client arriving. Postponing a "cold call" interview is important because there are many specific ways you should prepare for an interview, which would be impossible to do before the initial contact from the hiring committee. Often, the interviewer does not expect you to be available at that time but will expect to talk to you in the next day or so, so be ready to prepare for the interview quickly. Once your interview is arranged, remember that you should have the job advertisement, your application materials, and any other information you have gathered about the institution in front of you. It could be useful to have portable electronic access to such documentation stored on your laptop, telephone, or tablet if you need quick access or are out of town.

Academic Interview Format and Sample Questions

Most telephone interviews are conducted by a group of interviewers from the hiring committee. This will likely include the chair of the department, the chair of the search committee, and several other faculty members. Sometimes, undergraduate or graduate students are also involved (especially at teaching-oriented universities). Whereas the group of interviewers could include upward of eight to 10 people, one-on-one telephone interviews are not uncommon. Typically, four to seven interviewers are present. Most interviews last about 30 minutes, but some may be as short as 15 minutes or as along as an hour. The length is typically established before the interview or at the beginning of the phone call. Be aware that technology is prone to minor malfunctions and you could encounter a delay (from being on speaker phone), an echo effect, or some other electronic distraction. These issues will likely be experienced on both ends and for all candidates, so try to stay focused and use humor as appropriate (Career Advising and Planning Services, 2010). Your ability to "go with the flow" during these awkward times can speak volumes about your ability to handle unexpected situations, which occur frequently in academic and professional positions.

During the actual interview, the chair of the committee will typically first introduce the individuals participating in the interview and describe how the interview will be conducted. You can address the interviewers as they are introduced. In most cases, the departmental faculty will be introduced by their first names, but in some situations,

---

From the Trenches—Applicant Experiences and Advice

I did two telephone interviews and one of them didn't go very well and I never heard from them after that and one was much better. The one that didn't go well was particularly awkward because they didn't give any feedback on my responses and just went from one question to the next. It felt very formal. The second interview was more informal and they made comments after my responses so it felt more conversational.

—PhD in developmental psychology, assistant professor at a 4-year college

the department or institution may be more formal and refer to one another by title. In either case, follow the lead of the interviewing committee members (Career Advising and Planning Services, 2010). If in doubt, err on the side of being more formal, and wait for an invitation to be less formal. The interviewers may provide you with preliminary information about the institution and the position, but more often, they will launch right into the structured questions. Often, a different interviewer will ask each question, and frequently there will be little or no response provided for your answers, though occasional follow-up questions may be asked. One-on-one interviews or interviews that are less structured will usually flow much more smoothly, with the interviewer(s) providing feedback and information after each question before you are asked about another topic. Either way, it can be helpful to give yourself a moment after each question before you answer. You should avoid rushing to answer with the first example that comes to mind when a better example may occur to you shortly thereafter. It can be helpful to begin with "That's a great question" or "I'm glad you asked" and then begin to speak (Heiberger & Vick, 1999). If yours is a video interview, pause to take a drink before answering.

Video interviews are becoming more common with increasingly easy and accessible technology for online videoconferences. Thus, you should be prepared to do a videoconference (or Skype) interview. If you do not have these capabilities on your own computer, most institutions offer videoconferencing services to students for little or no cost. However, because web cameras are generally inexpensive, it would be a useful investment. The obvious difference between videoconference and telephone interviews is that videoconferencing enables the committee to see you, making physical presentation important. Remember to think about how you look as well as how the scene behind you looks. Make sure you dress for your video interview just as you would for an in-person interview (see Chapter 7, this volume). It is also important to look directly into the camera and make every effort to make eye contact (even if the video feed is choppy or blurry). It is good practice to address your answer to the person who asked the question. This could feel somewhat awkward; practicing ahead of time will make you feel more comfortable and confident (Potter, 2010).

To get the most out of your interview, it helps to spend some time thinking about what kinds of questions you might be asked, how to answer those questions, and what sorts of questions you would like to ask. Although you cannot be prepared for every question, you should anticipate and prepare for some standard ones. A typical set of interview questions for academic positions is presented in Exhibit 6.2. Do not be offended if search committee members ask you questions that you clearly answered in your submitted materials; many interviews are

EXHIBIT 6.2

Typical Interview Questions for Academic Positions

- Why are you interested in this institution or position?
- What courses could you teach here? (Check out the course offerings in the department ahead of time, and use actual course names to refer to the courses you could teach, as well as new courses you might propose.
- What sorts of research projects or topics could you pursue here? (In addition to preparing a discussion of your own research, find out the research interests of the faculty members in the department, and mention possible areas for potential collaboration or how your research possibly dovetails with theirs.)
- How will you or could you involve students in your research?
- What kinds of facilities would you need to conduct your research and teaching? (If possible, get a sense of what major items are already in place—such lists are often on departmental or college websites—and talk about how you could use what is there, as well as anything new you would need or want.)
- What questions do you have for us? (You should prepare several questions in advance. Asking these questions leads to more lively discussion among the interviewers and allows everyone's individual personalities to emerge.)

scripted and highly structured, and it is likely that at least a few of the members of the search committee will not have read your materials carefully or recently. Therefore, in your interview you will "need to convey a good deal of information about your work quickly, clearly, and efficiently" (Gamer & Krook, n.d., para. 2). You do not need write out a set of answers and memorize them word for word. However, you should think about the typical questions that are asked and decide what points you want to make and what stories you want to tell, according to the position for which you are applying. Stories drawn from experience are excellent answers to many questions but typically require preparation because they are challenging to think of on cue (Johnson, 2004). Stories could include a concrete example of a classroom strategy or a specific description of the results from a recent research project. Keep in mind that answering questions with specifics makes answers more interesting and credible (Johnson, 2004).

Generally, interview questions will ask you to address your interest in and potential contributions to the institution to which you are applying, your current and future research program, and your teaching experience and practice. Some typical general questions may arise also, particularly in longer interviews. You can use your background knowledge on the institution to make an educated guess about their likely line of questioning. However, although more teaching-oriented institutions will likely ask more questions about research, and research-oriented institutions will likely focus on research questions, be aware that research universities may also ask some questions about your teaching, and teaching-oriented institutions may ask about your research. Last, at the end of the interview be prepared for your interviewers to ask whether you have any questions for them. It is expected that you will have several prepared questions, and these can be just as important as the answers you provide to their questions. The questions you ask can tell the search committee what aspects of the job are most interesting to you, can let them know you did preliminary research on the institution (and now want to know more), and can help you to gain important information about the position to ascertain fit.

Many interviews will begin with the "why us–why you" type of question, which can be difficult to answer if you are not adequately prepared with specific information about the institution. Deviations of this line of inquiry include both questions about why you applied for or are interested in working at their institution as well as why you are particularly qualified for the position (i.e., why they would want you to work at their institution). In either case, this is an opportunity for you to convince the committee that you are a good fit. Your research on the department and institution becomes especially important here. Because this is a standard question, it is in your best interest to come up with three good, institution-specific reasons you are particularly excited about any position you interview for. In particular, you can mention potential areas of collaboration with faculty within or outside the department or involvement with ongoing initiatives or programs.

In any screening interview, it is typical to be asked a set of questions about your research. In this category, a standard question that should never take you by surprise is the generic "Tell us about your research." Although the question format may vary slightly, it is generally expected that you provide a brief description of your area of research along with recent projects you have completed or are currently working on (including your dissertation). This is where having written a research statement can come in handy, because you have already thought about how to succinctly describe your area of research and organize your topic areas. As with the research statement, keep in mind that you need to provide a clear explanation of your research program to nonexperts as well as convince the committee of its importance. Conveying excitement about your research and describing why your particular line of inquiry matters in your field should be an important component of your responses to questions about your research (Heiberger & Vick, 1999). Once you construct a 2- or 3-minute response that combines these elements, practice it in front of others so that you can naturally and convincingly provide it during your interview.

You will likely also be asked about your upcoming research projects, particularly those you would foresee pursuing if employed at their university. Because you should have an active research agenda shortly after assuming your academic position, you will likely be asked to briefly describe what that agenda might look like. You do not need to have definite plans or a fully conceptualized research proposal for your first project, but even preliminary plans indicate to the committee that you are thinking ahead and ready to pursue an independent program of research. If relevant, it can be useful to mention any plans you have to apply for grant funding, as well as any ongoing collaborative work in which you are engaged with colleagues at other institutions. It is important that the goals you describe are feasible or reasonable to pursue at the institution at which you are interviewing. It is also likely that the committee will want to know what kind of support you will need to pursue your research plans; for example, whether you will need specialized equipment, laboratory startup funds, special software, or travel money for archival research (UTSA University Career Center, 2010). Again, you should be careful about what you request during a preliminary interview. For example, if you are applying to work at a small teaching college, it is not appropriate to suggest that your dream research plan will require you to purchase your own functional magnetic resonance imaging machine.

At undergraduate institutions, such as liberal arts colleges, the committee will be particularly interested in how you can adapt your research to a small college setting while also providing undergraduate students with research opportunities. The committee may ask you to explain how you would get students excited about your research and to describe the specific aspects of your research in which students could participate. It can be useful to consider "how you will involve undergraduates in the process of intellectual inquiry that drives your research. How can you put questions and problems at the heart of your teaching, helping students formulate and test hypotheses even at the introductory level" (Armstrong, Stanton & Mannheimer, 2005, para. 16).

Most screening interviews will include several questions about teaching. You may be asked to talk about your teaching philosophy or what you believe are the qualities of an excellent instructor. These questions are often followed with a request for you to speak about how you practice your philosophy or how you embody some of the qualities you just outlined. Many committees will also ask you what you find rewarding and challenging about teaching and how you deal with the challenges. These questions can be difficult, particularly for inexperienced graduate students, and often require some forethought. Writing a teaching philosophy can be a helpful exercise for thinking about these questions, and it can be useful to review your teaching statement prior to a screening interview so that your ideas are fresh in your mind and relate to what the committee may have already read about you (see Chapter 4, this volume, for suggestions on creating these documents).

Be prepared to talk about what you can teach as well as what you would like to teach. Many people want to teach a graduate-level seminar on their dissertation topic, but you should remember that junior faculty in many departments mostly teach introductory courses. Most departments also offer "service" courses, such as special classes for nonmajors or large lecture courses that satisfy general education requirements; these may fill your teaching load. You will probably be required to teach courses at many different levels and should indicate your interest in doing so during the interview. Also, make sure that your responses are appropriate to the type of students at the interviewers' institution; you do not want to mention teaching a graduate level seminar at an institution that does not have any graduate students.

It is also likely that you will be asked to describe a course that you are expected to teach. Be ready to discuss how you would teach at least three undergraduate courses and one graduate seminar (if relevant). Most of these should be classes you know you will be expected to teach (particularly an introductory course in your area of the discipline), but one could be something special. For example, you could talk about a seminar drawing on your research expertise that would enhance the curriculum and that other candidates would not be able to offer. It is helpful to start with what you want students to learn from the course (i.e., learning objectives) and how that determines the curriculum and evaluation, and so on. You should make lists of the texts and/or materials you would use for each class and think about how you would present the material and the kinds of assignments you would create. This type of preparation is particularly important if you have minimal teaching experience. The more specific you can be when answering a question about teaching, the more you will appear ready to do the job.

Armstrong et al. (2005) provided detailed interview questions about teaching, explaining that it is likely you will be expected to talk about your teaching in the context of the classroom, including specific examples of how you will engage students and foster their learning:

- In large classes, will you lecture in a traditional way or incorporate active-learning strategies?
- What technologies do you anticipate using, and why (or why not)?
- How will you use small groups or in-class writing assignments to stimulate learning?
- How will you evaluate student learning both formally and informally throughout the semester?
- What kinds of exams, essays, reports, and other assignments do you find most effective in your field?
- How might a service-learning component enhance the learning experience for students?

Armstrong et al. (2005) also indicated that it is common for interviewees to be asked about the relationship—sometimes antagonistic, sometimes generative—between research and teaching. It can be useful to prepare a list of readings you would include in a graduate seminar in your specific area of expertise and be able to explain the aspects of your dissertation research or general research area that you could teach to undergraduates. This might also include addressing which ideas or assumptions would likely be challenging for them.

In some structured and in many unstructured interviews you will also be asked other general questions such as "What are your long-range plans and commitment to this department?" as well as questions about your comfort level with being located in the region or at a certain type of institution. For example, if you are from a major university in a large city and are interviewing at a liberal arts college in a small town, you should expect to be asked how you feel about such a transition. If you are interviewing at a religious institution, you may be questioned about how comfortable you are with their mission statement (Johnson, 2004). You may also be asked about service activities or your contributions to the campus community. Many committees will also ask about your commitment to and experiences working with diverse populations. For example, you may be asked, "How would you deal with the diversity of age, preparation, motivation, and backgrounds of your students?" or "What challenges does a culturally diverse classroom present to a teacher, and how do you meet these challenges?"

Questions to Ask Your Interviewers

One of the most important questions you will be asked during your screening interview is, "What questions do you have for us?" When you are looking for a faculty position, it is easy to forget that your job is to evaluate how well the position matches your needs. Having thoughtful and relevant questions prepared can draw attention to your preparation for the interview and indicate that you are genuinely interested in learning more about the position. Most important, it is only by asking questions that you will obtain the information that you need to decide whether the job is appropriate for you (Kuther, 2011). Depending on the length of the interview or time left in a scheduled interview, you should limit yourself to no more than five questions, but ask at least three. By having extra questions prepared, you can avoid asking about a topic that was already clearly covered during the interview. Asking questions shows that you are serious about the position and have done enough homework about the institution that you need more details as

EXHIBIT 6.3

Questions To Ask at the End of a Screening Interview

- What kinds of qualities are you looking for in a colleague?
- What are the interactions between faculty members like? Do they collaborate? Are there opportunities to discuss and share research?
- What is the expected teaching load each semester? Are any of these repeated sections?
- How large is the average "core" undergraduate psychology course? How large is the average upper division course?
- From where does the school draw its students (e.g., are they commuters or residents; are they from in or out of state; are they the traditional age, or are they returning students)?
- What kind of faculty and student growth is anticipated in the next 5 years?
- What type of job or career placement do the undergraduate students experience after graduation?
- What courses are to be taught by the person who is hired?
- What challenges are facing the department?
- What are the students' greatest strengths?
- How has the department changed in the last 5 to 10 years?
- Does the school support externships and international study?
- What is the school's relation to the community?

you consider your choices. For a list of possible questions you can ask at the end of an off-site interview, see Exhibit 6.3. More questions you can ask during the interview are described in Chapter 7, this volume.

Several considerations with regard to the questions you ask have become more important given the plethora of information available online. In general, it is best to avoid questions that ask about information easily attainable online (or any questions about specific benefits or salary; this information is typically provided at an on-site interview, and salary is typically discussed when you receive an offer). Schwebel and Karver (2004) recognized that "because applicants are expected to use the Internet to study departments they apply to, there is added expectation during interviews that applicants ask sophisticated questions to demonstrate their knowledge of an interest in the hiring department" (p. 175). Ultimately, you should ask questions that show you are already thinking about this particular institution and are excited by the prospect of working there. Keep in mind that regardless of the responses you get, be careful not to audibly react with surprise or dismay. This may indicate to the committee that you are not pleased with their response and are therefore not a good fit or not interested in the position.

The last question typically asked by candidates is about the next steps in the hiring process. Huang-Pollock and Mikami (2007) provided an example script for your closing statements:

> "I am sure that if I am invited to interview, I will have a lot more questions and that we will have a lot to talk about. My only

remaining question at this time is what is the process/time line from here?" Following the interviewer's response, you can close with, "Okay, that sounds terrific! I want to reiterate that I am very interested in your program, am excited about your interest in me, and hope to have an opportunity to visit to see if it is a good fit." (p. 105)

Energy and excitement at the close of an interview may be more important than you think; remember, the search committee is likely speaking to many candidates, so end the interview positively.

Preparing for Professional Interviews

Many of the same general recommendations hold for interviews for both academic and professional positions. In both types of interviews, you should be your strongest advocate and approach the conversation with confidence. However, Wagner (2000) noted the following:

> One issue that is particular to professional interviews is how you can serve as a compelling advocate for yourself and yet not come across as an overeducated snob who would never fit in the work team environment of that company. The best way to avoid seeming conceited while also supporting your qualifications is to prepare "success stories" to serve as responses to interviewers' questions. (para. 11)

The rest of this section offers guidance about off-site interviews that is specific to professional positions.

Given the amount of information available on the Internet about most organizations, it is imperative that before any interview you find out as much as possible about the organization to which you are applying. It is important to prepare for an interview by researching the company, organization, or agency and the specific position for which you are applying. In this way, you can anticipate possible lines of questioning, think through potential answers, and practice your responses. If there is a company mission or vision statement, memorize the key terms and ideas, and plan to incorporate in your interview responses the ways in which you fit into that mission. It can also be useful to determine the organizational structure and any "parent" companies or funders to the organization.

Beyond making you appear prepared for the interview and interested in the organization, prior research on the company and the position for which you applied is necessary to allow you to focus your interview responses on relating your skills, interests, and experiences to the needs of the organization and requirements of the position (Bock, 2005). As in academic job searches, reaching the interview stage means that you have passed the initial "screening" criteria. The hiring committee has determined that, on paper, you meet their basic criteria for the position, and they now want to see whether you can speak intelligently about your experiences and how you relate those experiences to the position for which you are applying. This can be challenging for many graduate students, who are often well versed in how they fit into academia but not as prepared to communicate clearly and effectively outside of that environment.

Beyond evaluating your qualifications, hiring committees for professional positions also assess how you might fit into the corporate culture, which means that your personal style is just as important as specific qualifications for the job:

> At every point in an interview, the employer is thinking about not just the roles and functions of the specific job for which you may be hired, but also for your potential to be promoted, your compatibility with other members of the work team, and your suitability as a representative of the company. (Wagner, 2000, para. 8)

Advance preparation for the position will help you develop the ability and confidence to skillfully emphasize your relevant skills and experiences.

Professional Interview Format and Sample Questions

One of the major differences between how you will be evaluated for a professional position versus an academic position is the emphasis on pragmatic rather than intellectual modes of thinking (Bradley, 2000). It is more common in industry interviews for a potential employer to ask questions about either behavioral matters ("Tell me about a time you had to deal with conflict in a work group") or situational matters ("What would you do if you knew you were going to be late on an important project?"):

> Once you have identified some success stories to use in response to these types of questions, think about the different ways in which you might use them to talk about a challenge or setback you faced, to highlight an important accomplishment, or to provide details on a specific experience listed on your résumé. (Wagner, 2000, para. 15)

Practice connecting these experiences with different skills relevant to the position for which you are applying.

Because the majority of graduate programs in psychology are preparing graduates to pursue careers in academia or in strictly clinical positions, many graduates from nonclinical fields of psychology may not recognize how their graduate training has developed skills relevant to professional positions. Newhouse (1998) reminded readers that research and teaching experiences as a graduate student also lead to the development of a host of underlying skills that are applicable to number of professional positions. For example, teaching requires one to be able to explain difficult concepts, organize materials into effective written or oral presentations, motivate students, and evaluate performance. Furthermore, the research and writing that is integral to producing a dissertation and graduating from a PhD program requires management skills and the ability to procure, develop, and organize resources; this "implies initiative, discipline, endurance, and optimism—not to mention all the research ability, writing skills, and substantive expertise involved" (Newhouse, para. 8). Finally, your experiences collaborating with your advisor or other graduate students are also useful skills to highlight because collaboration, particularly in writing, is an important component of work in professional settings (Bradley, 2000).

Several typical categories of questions are often asked in professional interviews. These include questions assessing your professional experiences; your working style with supervisors, administrators, and/or clients; specific knowledge you have of relevant content, materials, or treatments; and your understanding of the roles and responsibilities associated with the position. Some interviewers may also ask you to speak about personal qualities you possess that are relevant to the position for which you are applying, especially leadership skills and experience. A typical set of interview questions for professional positions is presented in Exhibit 6.4. As with academic interviews, also be prepared to ask questions at the end of the interview. These should be carefully planned ahead of time. You should follow up your interview by sending thank-you notes or e-mails.

One other element common with interviews for academic positions is the discussion of salary. It is widely agreed that job applicants should never bring up salary before the interviewer does; however, it is relatively common for employers to ask about your salary expectations during the interview (and they may follow up by asking what would encourage them to pay you more). Bradley (2001) offered several suggestions for responding to salary questions. First, she suggested avoiding the discussion until you are offered the position. For example, if asked to indicate what salary you expect, a possible response could be, "I am considering several different opportunities, and there are a number of factors to take into account. Would you mind giving me some idea of the salary range for this position?" If you cannot avoid a discussion of salary before you get an offer, Bradley recommended providing the

---

EXHIBIT 6.4

Typical Interview Questions for Professional Positions

- Why are you interested in this organization or position? (This is a particularly important question for nonprofit and public-service government positions that may pay less than private industry).
- What are your career goals, short-term and long-term?
- What do you consider to be your roles and responsibilities in this position? What training do you have in this area?
- What particular strengths or experiences, professional or personal, do you possess that qualify you for this position or will enhance your performance in this position? What areas you do still need to develop?
- Describe your internship and research experiences. What are some of the most significant things you learned?
- What should a supervisor expect from someone in your position? What are you looking for in your supervisor or manager?
- How would you describe your working style? What kind of work environment are you most comfortable with?
- Anticipate at least one question that assesses knowledge of content relevant to your area of psychology or the position. For example, a clinical psychologist may be asked to reflect on and suggest a treatment plan for a case study, a school psychologist may be asked about best practices for working with children with a particular learning disability, and a research consultant could be asked to describe the steps he or she took to successfully complete a large project.

---

employer with a wide salary range based on research on current salaries for similar positions in similar locations. Another option would be to state at the outset any salary requirements you have, because it would be a waste of both your time and the potential employer's time to go through the interview and/or negotiation process if your required salary is not feasible to the organization.

Following Up

After the interview, you should send a thank-you e-mail or letter to the chair of the search committee or individually to each faculty member who interviewed you. It should be a brief, simple message to thank them for taking the time to speak with you. You can use the opportunity to relay your enthusiasm for the position, and you can tell them that you look forward to meeting them in the future. For professional positions, following up can also include linking your profile to the organization on LinkedIn, following them on Twitter, or associating yourself with them on Facebook (as long as your profile is job-friendly), all of which

---

From the Trenches—Employer Experiences and Advice

Do a ton of research before going in for an interview. Know the courses typically taught in the department to which you are applying. I have had interviewees act surprised when it is mentioned that they have to do quite a bit of service work for tenure at our institution. It's a kiss of death if an applicant thinks they will teach 15 credits a semester and have to do nothing else. It's also bad when applicants act surprised when we mention that they must teach at least one night course. That tells me that they did not read or remember the ad to which they applied. Another mistake that I have seen is when applicants make assumptions about community college students. They assume they are all ethnic minorities and poor. Diversity, which we have in spades, is broader than what many applicants think it is. Don't feel that you need to know all the answers about local culture. You can't. That stuff is not on websites. Be humble and make it clear that you are willing to learn how things go at a specific institution while at the same time making it clear that you have full confidence over what you do know.

—PhD in developmental psychology
at a community college in the Northeast

---

can easily be reversed if you are not selected for the position. Waiting to hear the hiring committee's decision is difficult, but be patient. It is best not to annoy the chair or the members of the search committee by asking about the status of the search.

If you are not offered the position, it may be possible to ask someone on the committee about aspects of your interview that could be improved; however, many human resources departments discourage individuals from speaking candidly about the search process. It is also important not to take a rejection personally. It can be difficult to know exactly what will be evaluated positively or negatively during a screening interview. "People often don't get the job when they think they absolutely nailed the interview; sometimes people who feel like they totally flunked the interview get the job offer" (Trabb, 2007, Reply #7).

The Bottom Line: Top Recommendations for New Doctorates

Preparation is the key to a successful interview. Especially important is finding out more about the position for which you will be interviewed and the institution to which you applied. Most off-site interviews follow a similar format, including a set of predetermined questions about your interest in their position and institution; your program of research; and your teaching experience, interests, and practices. In your responses, you should highlight specific examples of the points you are making. Remember that otherwise good communicators can falter during phone interviews, because the body language used to evaluate interest is obscured (Jenkins, 2008). The best way to avoid mistakes during your interview is to be as prepared as possible. Having a general idea of what you might be asked will allow you to develop concise and informative answers in advance. Last, during off-site interviews you will frequently be asked for your own questions, which you should prepare ahead of time and amend as needed on the basis of what was already covered in the interview.

On-Site Interviews and Job-Related Talks

7

Before jumping into the details of interviews and job talks for academic and professional positions, it is important to recognize the overarching purpose behind an on-site interview. A search or hiring committee already knows about an applicant's clinical practice experience, courses taught, and manuscripts submitted for publication from the curriculum vitae and the cover letter; the purpose of the interview, however, is to determine what you are like in person (Feldman & Silvia, 2010). Interviews allow search committees to get a glimpse of who you are, what you think of yourself, and how you treat others. Because you have the potential to be a member of their practice, clinic, department, or organization for years, perhaps decades, the hiring decision is a critical choice.

Because your disposition and personality are being evaluated, it is important to remember that the entire time you are on-site (and before and after that period too) you are being interviewed. How you interact with staff, clients, or students in the hallway or elevator will be noted and likely discussed. If you have an alcoholic beverage at dinner, it will be noted by some (though others will care less). Although it is normal to concentrate on the formal interview itself (e.g., job talk, individual meetings with potential supervisors), every moment on site is part of the interview (Kuther, 2008).

From the Trenches—Employer Experiences and Advice

Don't act too comfortable or casual during the noninterview process (e.g., during a meal). Don't drink too much! We may have two glasses of wine, but you shouldn't, particularly if you can't handle it. Maintain professionalism throughout the whole time. Don't share personal information unless it's asked for or it presents itself as a bonding opportunity (e.g., "Oh, you have twins? So do I!" "I see you use Google Calendar. I do too! Isn't it wonderful for keeping you organized?")

—Kelly J., PhD in social psychology, assistant professor at a private college in the Northeast

Informal conversations you have will be vital to how the hiring committee perceives you and your fit with their institution or organization. Sternberg (2003) offered conversational suggestions, such as to be your own press agent and not to undersell yourself. Exhibit 7.1 presents some considerations about communication skills in job interviews.

Your preparation for the job interview may be taken as an indicator of how you will prepare for the daily tasks of the job. Think about what you can offer the department and the immediate contributions you could offer from your first day there. Find out before your visit who the search committee members are; that is, do your homework. Be genuinely interested in those who are interviewing you, and be interested in the university or company to which you are applying. Remember to dress comfortably but respectfully. If you are invited to a casual restaurant to which you would normally wear jeans, choose a neater alternative instead—something that is less casual than jeans but more casual than a suit. Finally, we recommend that you be yourself, and let the committee see the real you. If, during the interview, you portray someone other than the real you, and this "fake" you gets hired, you could end up being miserable in the position because the perceived "match and fit" was a charade.

Caplan (1993) offered some interview advice for female applicants, but in fact her advice makes good sense for all job applicants: (a) Pretend to be your own press agent, and do not undersell your skills and abilities because of a lack of confidence; (b) be aware that it is likely that many, if not most, members of the search committee will be white males; (c) be aware that sometimes interviews and job talks are not about the applicant but about current faculty members jostling for position in the department; (d) remember to dress comfortably but respectfully, in a manner befitting the typical job talk; (e) ask people in your network about working conditions in the department for which you are being interviewed, and try to ask undergraduate or graduate students

EXHIBIT 7.1

What the Literature Says . . . About Communication Skills and Gender Differences in Job Interviews

As you can imagine, there are experts in every field imaginable related to human behavior, including researchers who study the job interview process, or what is more formally called *oral proficiency interviews*. A fascinating study conducted by Goldberg and Cohen (2004) examined how gender differences combine with nonverbal and verbal communication skills to affect the oral proficiency interview, especially in decision making. These authors noted that although résumés are still a critical component of the job application process, applicants can improve their odds of success in the job search with verbalizations and nonverbal cues. Their research was completed at three schools in Southeastern United States as part of campus recruiting interviews. Although not identical to the new doctorate job talk, similarities do exist between the interview conditions. An assessment rubric was developed by Goldberg and Cohen that included questions about whether the applicant would be invited for an on-site interview, whether the applicant would probably be offered the job, and whether the company would definitely consider this applicant for the position. The data presented here are based on recorded (and then scored) dyads between 41 recruiters and 210 applicants, which yielded 311 usable dyads.

A complicated set of results emerged from this research. As predicted, both verbal and nonverbal interview skills are significantly positively related to interview assessments. In considering the strength of these relationships, nonverbal skills were a significantly better predictor than verbal skills (opposite to what Goldberg & Cohen, 2004, predicted). It was expected that a Verbal/Nonverbal × Gender interaction would emerge, but that was not the case. Marginally significant outcomes indicated that for men and women with low to moderate nonverbal skills, there were no significant differences in interview assessments, but men with high nonverbal skills received the highest assessment scores of any group or group combination. Overall, applicants who "looked the part" in their job pursuits, compared with those who did not, demonstrated positive verbal and nonverbal behaviors. Further, nonverbal skills were a stronger predictor of verbal skills in the overall interview assessments. The interview process includes many layers of complexity for both applicants and assessors.

there what the school is like; and (f) be aware that personal questions unrelated to job performance are illegal, and you do not have to answer them (suggestions on how to handle these situations are found at the end of this chapter).

Before You Go

As with off-site interviews, an integral part of preparing for an on-site interview is doing as much homework as you can on the position and institution or company to which you are applying. Typically, this involves looking online for information about, for example, the mission statement, recent news and events, and even the administrative structure. It is also helpful to do some research into the community in which the institution or organization is located, particularly if you are not familiar with the town or state. For academic institutions, you should examine the department website to learn about their program and courses offered as well as the individual faculty members. When possible, do some research on the publications and presentations of current faculty members; this might include contacting members of your network of professional contacts and/or searching PsycINFO or Google. For professional positions, know the names of people who hold important roles in the organization (including board members), look for information about recent contracts the company has held, and review publicly available reports and company products.

When setting up the interview, make sure you extract all the information you can about the expectations for you while on site (e.g., where you will stay, transportation arrangements, who you will be meeting with). It is especially important to find out about the job talk expectations (discussed later in the chapter; Darley & Zanna, 2004). Be prepared to be asked for a title for your job talk or teaching presentation when you are arranging your visit. Even though it may be tentative, try to be as accurate as possible. If possible, find out who the search committee members are or who will be making the key decisions about hiring; academic search committees typically comprise four faculty members, and a few also include students (undergraduate or graduate) or faculty from other departments (Sheehan, McDevitt, & Ross, 1998).

In applying for academic positions, the match and fit of your personality with the existing personalities in the department, your research

---

From the Trenches—Applicant Experiences and Advice

I'm sure it's important to be prepared, for the job talk in particular (this is an area you can control), and for likely interview questions, and to know as much as you can about the place you are interviewing at. For me, though, the best thing I think I did was accept the fact that I could not possibly prepare for every question, and I would likely forget some information about the site. I let go of control and tried to be in the moment. I also didn't try to impress the site; I tried to answer questions completely and honestly, while still being professional. My biggest surprise about the process was how frequently I was expected to ASK questions, not answer them. There were several individual interviews where no questions were asked of me at all, and the person was just offering their opinions and advice. So my biggest piece of advice would be to generate as many questions as you can, and don't hesitate to ask the same questions to multiple people.

—PhD in psychology at large university in the Southeast

interests in the context of departmental emphases, and what you can teach compared with what is needed are all important considerations. If you have been invited to an on-site interview, you are deemed to be qualified for the job, because a department would not waste the resources or the time (yours or theirs) to pay for someone to visit who does not appear to be a good match and fit with their needs. For a professional position, the same principles apply. Employers are looking for specific skills or expertise that can contribute to their organization. For example, do you bring skills or a theoretical orientation that is not represented in the current practice but is desired? Is your background similar to the direction in which the organization is hoping to go? It is difficult to determine whether or not you are suited for a position when you read about it in an advertisement. Although it becomes clearer after an off-site interview, the on-site interview is the final determinant of whether the position is suited to you. In fact, if you depart from that interview wondering whether you are indeed a match and fit for the position and location, then you probably are not.

ENVISION YOURSELF WORKING THERE

One way to help establish a perception of fit is to set your conversations and presentations in an "If I were here . . ." framework. Picture yourself working in that particular clinic, hospital, government agency, office, or academic department. What would you do if you were there? Can you see yourself initiating child and adolescent play therapy groups because while reviewing materials provided by the practice, you noted a high amount of referrals for child adjustment issues resulting from recent parental divorce? Or if a department that previously had a heavy emphasis on undergraduate teaching is now switching to a heavier research emphasis, and in graduate school you had experience training and supervising undergraduate research assistants, think of how valuable you would be to that department. Do you picture yourself living in that town or city? Do you picture yourself interacting with these colleagues for the next few years and perhaps longer? Approaching conversations, formal interviews, and your job talk with this mentality will help you visualize yourself in the position and may help the hiring committee visualize you at their institution or organization as well.

CONSIDER LOGISTICS AND ATTIRE

Last, there are some logistics to consider before embarking on your travels. Although you may have minimal control over your travel plans, it is useful to make your arrangements as far in advance as possible. This includes not only flight plans and hotel reservations but also transportation to and from the airport (including directions, if you are driving yourself), to and from the campus or organization, and to and from dinners. Typically, the organization or department administrative assistants will do this for you, but you should be informed as plans are being made. It is also good to be aware that although almost all organizations or institutions will pay for your visit, some will expect you to make your own travel arrangements, for which they will reimburse you. Some organizations or institutions will require you to pay back any nonrefundable travel costs if you decide not to attend their on-site interview (e.g., if you accept another position).

In preparing to leave for your interview, you should also think about your attire. Often, you will spend at least 1, if not 2, days on your feet during the on-site interview. As such, you should plan to wear professional and comfortable clothes (and shoes). Other logistical considerations include making sure that your duties as an intern, teaching assistant, or instructor are covered while you are away; planning enough padding in your travel schedule in case of weather or technical delays; getting enough rest before you leave; and making sure that you have all the materials you need for your interview printed out and organized before you leave, especially because some interview meetings may be scheduled before you have time to check into your hotel. It is also a good idea to wear professional clothing while traveling so that you will not have to attend your interview in jeans if your luggage gets lost in transit. For this reason, it is also often suggested that you carry your bags onto the flight with you instead of checking them.

PREPARE SOME QUESTIONS FOR YOUR PROSPECTIVE EMPLOYER

One of the elements of the on-site interview that many candidates are unprepared for is the need to ask questions of your interviewers. Although you may expect to have long meetings with faculty members or program directors to answer a list of questions they have prepared for you, it is common for them to ask you what questions you have for them. If you are not prepared for this ahead of time, the meeting could be quite uncomfortable. Often, you will be expected to ask questions during more informal meetings as well, such as during the ride from the airport to the hotel, at a meal or during a coffee break, and when touring the campus.

Many sources provide good suggestions for interview questions to ask prospective employers. Brown (2009) and Darley and Zanna (2004) suggested several aspects of the job that are appropriate for applicants to ask about during on-site interviews. First, although some information can be obtained ahead of time through the departmental website, demographic questions about the department can provide useful information. For example, what are the students like? How many majors are there? Are they interested in research assistantships and/or teaching assistantships? How many students go on to graduate school? What kinds of positions do graduate students usually take after graduation? It is also appropriate to ask faculty members about their current research projects, though a lack of knowledge about each faculty member's research area can make it appear as if you did not do your homework ahead of time.

Sowers-Hoag and Harrison (1998) suggested asking about resources or support you will need; for example, library resources, computer and software resources, teaching resources such as academic technology or a center for teaching excellence, laboratory space, and funds available for travel, statistical consulting, or specialized equipment. It can be useful to think about what is available to you at your home institution and whether those resources are available at the place you are interviewing. It is also appropriate to ask about workload issues, such as the number of clients you are expected to have, what the teaching load is, how many teaching or research assistants will be available to you, and what the requirements for service are. However, remember that your verbal and nonverbal responses to such information should be neutral to positive. At the end of your interview or shortly after it is over, you should inquire about the decision-making process.

At academic institutions, it is also common to receive (or ask for) information about tenure policies and specifically what the research expectations are for tenure. For example, how are annual evaluations handled? Is there a 3-year review? What is the process for applying for tenure? Is it possible to apply for tenure early? What are the criteria for awarding tenure? How many publications per year are needed to make progress toward tenure? How are conference presentations valued, as well as published abstracts, technical reports, and other non–peer-reviewed materials? Are start-up funds available for a lab? Are there restrictions on what start-up money can be spent on or when it must be spent by? Are there internal grant opportunities? Are there expectations for external grant activity? Are there support mechanisms available to assist in the grant application process? What about post-grant support? These questions can be asked of provosts, deans, and department chairs, but it can also be useful to ask them of recently tenured faculty as well as newer faculty members to get perspectives from individuals currently dealing with these types of issues. Taking a list of questions to an interview and referring to it during breaks or even during meetings can be an excellent method for approaching this important element of your interview. A comprehensive list of basic questions (primarily for academic positions) is provided in Exhibit 7.2; think ahead of time about whom you might ask which questions.

EXHIBIT 7.2

General Interview Questions

- What is the size of the department?
- What is the structure of the department (e.g., different tracks, disciplines)?
- What is the number of faculty at each rank?
- What are the department's future expansion (or contraction) plans?
- What is the department's standing within the university?
- How are graduate students matched with faculty?
- How are graduate admissions handled, in general?
- How long does it typically take graduate students to finish the program?
- Does the graduate program have both master's and doctoral students or just one or the other?
- For clinical psychologists, what is the relative emphasis on research versus clinical work?
- What is the relationship between subdisciplines or areas within the department?
- What is the relationship between the psychology department and other departments?
- Are any of the faculty members in private practice? Are there any guidelines with respect to private practice or consulting?

Responsibilities

- What is the teaching load?
- Is there any reduction in teaching load during the first year?
- Is there any reduction in teaching load for departmental service? For grants?
- Can you buy out of teaching with grants?
- Is summer teaching expected?
- What proportion of the junior faculty is tenured?
- What are the expectations for tenure?
- What are the expectations with regard to committee work?

Resources

- How much lab space can one expect? Where will it be?
- How are research assistants and teaching assistants assigned?
- How are resources such as administrative assistants, photocopying, postage, long-distance calling, and parking handled?
- What kinds of computer equipment and support can one expect?
- What library services are available?
- What kinds of mentorship are available for junior faculty?

Benefits

- What kinds of travel funds are available from the department?
- What kinds of medical, dental, and retirement plans are offered by the university?
- Are there opportunities for summer funding?
- What is a typical starting salary?

Grants and Research

- What are the university's expectations with regard to obtaining outside grant funding?
- What kinds of internal grant funding are available?
- What kinds of participant populations are available? Is there a subject pool?
- Is there an office of sponsored research in the university or college?
- How much time is typically available for research?
- What is the quality of the students, and might they reasonably become involved in research?

EXHIBIT 7.2 *(Continued)*

Location

▪ What real-estate opportunities are available?
▪ What is the cost of living?
▪ Is there any university assistance with mortgages?

Faculty Relations

▪ Are relations between junior faculty and senior faculty cordial?
▪ Is collaboration among faculty encouraged (or discouraged)?
▪ Why do people decide to come to the university? Why do some people not decide to come?

Note. Adapted from *Internships in Psychology: The APAGS Workbook for Writing Successful Applications and Finding the Right Fit* (2nd ed., p. 105) by C. Williams-Nickelson, M. J. Prinstein, and W. G. Keilin (Eds.), 2008, Washington, DC: American Psychological Association. Copyright 2008 by the American Psychological Association.

PREPARE YOUR JOB TALK

Feldman and Silvia (2010) suggested two things to consider when focusing on your job talk: (a) the job talk is not really about research, teaching, or your theoretical orientation, and (b) it is important to know the composition of the audience and their expectations. What is the goal of your talk? Is it for you to teach a mock class on the topic of your dissertation? Will there be undergraduates and graduate students there or just graduate students plus departmental faculty? If you are giving a talk for a professional position, will all the practice partners be there in addition to office staff and/or interns? Try to elicit from your contact person what the overt and covert goals are during the job talk. It is also appropriate to find out what technology will be available to you. For example, are you expected to bring your own laptop? Will there be Internet access? Be sure to prepare multiple methods of accessing your electronic presentation in case you cannot retrieve it from your e-mail or server. Be prepared for the technology to fail; bring printed copies of your slides, notes, and handouts if they will be required for your audience to follow the presentation. Also be aware that job talks will occasionally be audio- or videotaped for committee members who are not able to attend.

Although originally intended as advice for science job talks, Delph (2010) offered helpful rules for such talks that apply to new doctorates in psychology as well (see Exhibit 7.3). Although you do not need to follow such rules precisely, think about why you would choose to not follow any of the particular rules. Also think about the difficulty of anticipating audience expectations; if you are unclear about the expected focus of your on-site interview, then perhaps following these rules at first may be prudent, and as you become more proficient, decide which rules can be broken. While you are still completing your

EXHIBIT 7.3

Guidelines for the Job Talk

- Begin with a clear, concise introduction. Your introduction should include an outline of the material you will cover.
- Be sure to begin discussing your data within the first 20 minutes of the presentation.
- Discuss your methods only briefly as necessary to qualify your results. Do not dwell on the minutia of your methods or statistics. Establish that your methods were logical, and move on with your talk.
- It is not necessary to discuss sample sizes, assuming your data is significant.
- Your slides should be legible, even from a distance, and should not contain too much information. Overly cluttered slides obscure your results and may confuse or bore your audience.
- Do not include slides intended to remind you to discuss something. Instead, practice the talk enough that you do not require external reminders.
- Do not read what is on the slide to your audience. They can read. Slides should summarize for the audience what you are discussing at that time.
- Avoid mentioning subjects you do not plan to discuss, especially early in the talk.
- Practice your talk, so that you are comfortable being yourself when delivering it.
- Exhibit your enthusiasm for your research topic.
- Be mindful of your time limit. Time your presentation, and make sure you allow for interruptions and questions at the end of your talk. If your seminar does not begin on time, adjust your talk to fit.
- Do not draw out your presentation to fit the time allotted. If you can summarize your work clearly and completely in less than the time given, do so. Your audience will appreciate your concision.
- Summarize and end your talk clearly. Indicate that you have reached the end, and seek questions from your audience.

doctorate, try to attend job interview talks on campus for academic positions and at a practice or business location for professional positions. The latter suggestion may be more difficult to effect, but even attending a half dozen academic job talks will provide some feedback about dos and don'ts.

CREATE YOUR TAG LINE OR ELEVATOR TALK

It cannot be emphasized enough how important your two-sentence description of what you do and your 5-minute "elevator talk" (your "spiel") are. It is your chance to deliver your message in a concise package and to be memorable. If you are interviewing with partners in the hope of joining a group practice, you should try to provide them with retrievable cues so that when they discuss the applicants, positive characteristics about you will help you stand out from the crowd. If you are looking for a tenure-track assistant professor position, when the department chair proposes to the dean that they hire you, you want the dean to remember you and be on your side ("Oh yes, she's the social psychologist who studies how children learn to interact with and appreciate the esthetics of the environment—I liked her"). That "tag line" about your specialty and what you study are the parts of the elevator talk that you want remembered.

Interview Tips for Academic Positions

On-campus interviews are of varying length and include a variety of activities. Typically, you will be expected to participate in a full-day interview that occasionally includes half-day activities when you arrive or leave (e.g., dinner, a brief morning meeting). Some institutions have 2 full interview days. During this time, some standard types of meetings and activities occur. You will likely meet with a department chair, dean, or provost; receive campus and building tours; talk with faculty and staff individually or in group interviews; have formal or informal time to meet with current students; and give a job talk and/or teaching presentation (Sheehan, McDevitt, & Ross, 1998). Meals will also be scheduled and will usually include several faculty members. In general, you should be informed of the expected length of the visit and itinerary before you arrive (although often you receive a finalized version only a day or two ahead of time, and it can be subject to change). Figure 7.1 provides an example itinerary for an academic position at a liberal arts college.

In a survey of 98 search committee chairs, Sheehan, McDevitt, and Ross (1998) found that the most important criteria used to evaluate candidates at their interview were (in order) their performance at an interview with the search committee, their performance during a research talk or colloquium, their performance during an undergraduate lecture, their ability to get along with other faculty members, their personality, and, last, their performance at an interview with the department chair. Through this somewhat grueling process, be confident. Think about what you can offer the department; that is, how will you proceed if you were offered the job and accepted it? What immediate contribution could you make? How will you make yourself invaluable to the ongoing efforts as well as the new directions that a department may be considering? If you can focus on several key points during each of your meetings, it will help you stay focused and ensure you provide a consistent message about your qualifications. "Keep in mind that for most applied positions the employer will be evaluating clinical skills by the breadth of practical experience that the candidate has. Hence, a real familiarity with one's practicum and internship experiences should be demonstrated" (Levendusky, 1986, p. 12).

FIGURE 7.1

Campus Visit of

Jesse Velazquez

Developmental Psychology Candidate—Monday, January 16, 2012

Time	Sunday, January 15, 2012	Place
Departing Dallas @ 6:20 a.m. to arrive at Boston @ 12:33 p.m.	Call 1-800-555-1827 for exact pick up location to meet Town car service. Confirmation #16723 Check into Marriott Courtyard.	Marriott Courtyard Boston, MA
5:30 p.m.	Dinner with Karen Smith, Bill Jones, and Margie Hanson	A committee member will pick you up.
	Monday, January 16, 2012	
7:45 a.m.	Drew Lowe will pick you up for drive to campus.	
8:00–9:15 a.m.	Breakfast with Drew Lowe	Student Union
9:15–10:00 a.m.	Meet with psychology faculty members—Fran Johnson, Margie Hanson, and Melissa Cortez	PB-315
10:00–10:30 a.m.	Karen Smith	Java Cafe
10:30 a.m.	Break	
10:45–11:45 a.m.	Presentation	MP-118
12:00–1:30 p.m.	Lunch with Bill Jones, Margie Hanson, and Elisa Wu	
1:45–2:30 p.m.	Margie Hanson	MP-214
2:30–3:00 p.m.	Elisa Wu and Chris Adams—Tour	Campus

Example Campus Visit Interview Itinerary

FIGURE 7.1 *(Continued)*

3:00–3:30 p.m.	Meet with Chris, Elisa, and other students	
3:30–4:00 p.m.	Susan Martin	AB-223
4:15–5:00 p.m.	Richard Ramos	AB-227
5:00–5:15 p.m.	Drew Lowe—Follow Up	PB-210
5:30 p.m. Town Car Pickup	Depart Campus in Town Car Conf # 17445 for Logan United Flt 0273 @ 8:10 p.m. Leave from behind Psychology Building parking lot.	

Dr. Susan Martin	**President**
Dr. Richard Ramos	**Vice President for Academic Affairs, Dean of Faculty, and Professor of Engineering**
Dr. Drew Lowe	**Chair, College of Arts and Sciences, Professor of Psychology**
Dr. Fran Johnson	**Department Chair, Psychology, Professor of Psychology**
Dr. Margie Hanson	**Associate Professor of Psychology**
Dr. Karen Smith	**Assistant Professor of Literature**
Elisa Wu	**Student**
Chris Adams	**Student**

Example Campus Visit Interview Itinerary

QUESTIONS YOU MAY BE ASKED DURING AN INTERVIEW

We have reviewed questions that you could ask your interviewers during an interview. We now turn the discussion to the types of questions you will likely have to answer in an on-site interview for an academic position. Usually, the types of questions asked during on-campus interviews are similar to those asked during a phone interview (reviewed more extensively in the previous chapter): You will often be asked why you are interested in the position in addition to questions about your research, teaching, and service experiences. You might find that in comparison with phone interviews, on-campus interviews are more conversational and unstructured and more detailed (especially because follow-up questions can be asked). In addition, you will be expected to tailor your answers more specifically to the institution than during a telephone interview. Furthermore, because you will interact socially with your interviewers, you are likely to be asked more personal questions (e.g., What are your hobbies? Do you like the theater? Do you like to ski? Do you have any pets?). Rather than directly contributing

---

From the Trenches—Employer Experiences and Advice

Eagerness to demonstrate knowledge sometimes comes across as rudeness when the candidate interrupts questions to provide answers. Many candidates are familiar with only their own institution's way of doing things and may belittle our methods without knowing the history behind decisions. A lack of familiarity with faculty research, classes offered, or general knowledge about the department is often taken as a lack of interest.

—PhD in psychology, associate professor

---

to hiring decisions, these questions are usually asked to make conversation and to provide you with information about the community and surrounding area that might be enticing to you and your family. A sampling of the types of questions you should be prepared to answer when applying for a counseling or clinical-oriented position is provided in Exhibit 7.4.

EXHIBIT 7.4

Sample Interview Questions for a Clinical or Counseling Position

---

- Why do you want this job?
- Why are you considering leaving your present counseling position?
- Tell me about yourself.
- What special training or skills do you possess?
- What is your experience level in this particular field of counseling?
- Describe your strengths and weaknesses.
- If offered, how long might you stay with us?
- What theoretical approach to counseling do you take?
- How do you handle conflict?
- What theoretical supervisory approach do you work from?
- What are your professional goals? What do you see yourself doing 5–10 years from now?
- Who has been the most influential person in your life, and why?
- What is your experience working with at-risk youth?
- Regarding research, what is you specialty area?
- Why did you leave your last position?
- What salary would you expect to receive?
- What drew your interest to the advertised position here?
- What do you think are the greatest challenges for our field in the next 10 years?
- What professional organizations are you a member of?
- How have you or how would you support multiculturalism in your practice?
- What additional training do you have, if any?
- Why should I hire you?
- What other questions do you have for me?

Note. Data from Hodges and Connelly (2010).

THE JOB TALK

The on-site job talk is typically the most important component of the on-site job interview (Brown, 2009). A good research job talk will hopefully answer the following questions: (a) What problem did I address? (b) Why would anyone work on this problem? (c) What is significant about what I have done? and (d) How has my work made progress in solving the problem (University of Nebraska—Lincoln, 2011)? For the structure of your talk, plan on following the logical storytelling pattern that an American Psychological Association manuscript follows: introduction, method, results, and discussion or conclusions. Present your own data if you can, but if you cannot, make sure you present some data (or data outcomes) with proper citations (Brown, 2009). Also think about these suggestions for timing and structure offered by the University of Nebraska—Lincoln (2011):

- Background (15 minutes): Material understandable to everyone in the room.
- Your approach (10 minutes): Material understandable to people in the field.
- Your outcomes (10 minutes): Material understandable to experts in your field.
- Summary (10 minutes): Material understandable to everyone in the room.

Be precise with your story and make sure to end with a take-away message that makes sense, matters, and is memorable. What does your work contribute to both the discipline and the human condition? Why should a department want to fund this research? In other words, answer the "so what" questions: Why does your research matter? Why is your research important? "Leave the audience with a take-home message about your purpose, what you tried to show, what it meant, and why they should care" (Kuther, 2008, p. 241).

It is expected that you will leave enough time for questions at the end of the talk. You might be tempted to use the whole time so as to avoid questions because you are afraid of being stumped. This is not a good strategy. If you cannot follow the instructions on the preparation for a talk that is preplanned in a fixed time slot, you may not be perceived as a good candidate for a position at that institution. The best approach to answering tough questions is to be honest with the data. If you do not know the answer to a question, do not make up an answer; say you do not know. You may speculate about the answer, but make it clear that you are doing so ("I don't have any data to support this claim, but here's what I think is going on . . ."). Be confident and defend your research, but also be aware and respectful of

---

From the Trenches—Employer Experiences and Advice

I remember one candidate that said "um" 216 times in a 30-minute job talk. I almost quit counting, but I wanted to see how many times a person could continue on with "um" after almost every other word. A job talk that is not presented in front of a candidate's core faculty at least four or five times before going on an interview is a recipe for disappointment. Of course, this does not count the 10 to 15 times a candidate should have rehearsed the presentation prior to presenting to the core faculty.

—PhD in social psychology, professor

---

differing viewpoints. Disagreements about theories or interpretations of the data may occur, but always remain civil, and do not be argumentative; being respectful and collegial will serve you well in the long run (Sternberg, 2003). Some audiences will ask questions they genuinely are interested in hearing the answers for, whereas others may be "testing" you. There are also occasions when faculty members in the audience may be asking a question to make themselves look good in front of colleagues, and the questions asked may have little relevance to you.

In their survey of 98 department chairs, Sheehan et al. (1998) found that typical job talk blunders included being disorganized, being uninspiring, being poorly timed, and lacking knowledge of research design. To avoid these errors, practice your job talk in front of others and take it seriously, including the feedback you are given. Did the story follow logically? Did you share enough of your personality for audience members to get a glimpse of the real you? The more you can practice and prepare for what is expected, the more confidence you will have on those occasions when the unexpected occurs. You should also sit in on as many job talks as you can in your own academic department so that you can begin to assimilate common practices and observe the trouble spots that other applicants tend to have during a job talk.

Being cognizant of the logistics for your talk is also important. When setting up your schedule for an on-site interview that includes a job talk, try to find out what kind of talk you are expected to give and to what audience. Is it meant to be a research-style conference talk aimed at faculty, or is it aimed at undergraduate students? Is it meant to be a guest lecture in an introductory or upper division class? In general, you should plan on using PowerPoint (Darley & Zanna, 2004) and anticipate that the department will provide the needed technology. However, it is best to bring your own so that you can rehearse your talk the night before (Brown, 2009). You should also prepare for the possibility that the technology will fail, so you should bring with you multiple copies of your presentation in a variety of formats.

Interview Tips for Professional Positions

The final stages of job searches for professional positions typically include an on-site interview that will be composed of individual interviews, committee interviews, group or panel interviews, lunch interviews, and more informal meeting periods. During these meetings, you will be interviewed by individuals on the hiring committee, who likely hold positions at higher ranks than the position you are applying for (e.g., senior consultants, program directors, senior researchers, presidents, CEOs). You may also be interviewed by the individual you are replacing (if he or she is leaving the organization amicably). Be prepared to answer questions about your qualifications, relevant work experience, career goals, and leadership and teamwork skills. Interviewers are likely to ask you why you are the best candidate for the position; they will also want to know about how your experience with activities, topics, and clients is directly related to the position (e.g., developing quality research methods, statistics, presenting data to clients), how well you work with competing deadlines and shifting priorities, how well you work in a team, and how you would respond to various problems that may arise. You will likely be asked to speak about your strengths and weaknesses as well.

It is important to be aware of some of the common misconceptions among nonacademic professional organizations about PhDs, including the perception that they are not able to or are not interested in doing applied research, that they will not be good team players, that they cannot communicate in simple or direct terms, or that they are only pursuing the position as a last resort (i.e., they would rather be in academia). Be prepared to address these concerns directly if asked, and take opportunities throughout the interview to reinforce your interest in the organization and its work. Last, keep in mind that image may be especially important when interviewing at a company or organization for a position that involves client contact; be sure to present yourself professionally in what you wear, what you say, and how you carry yourself.

Unlike academic applicants, applicants for applied clinical positions are likely to meet with an interdisciplinary team (Humphrey & Kang, 2009; Levendusky, 1986). Perhaps even more so than their academic counterparts, professional applicants will be subject to "match and fit" scrutiny, but the criteria may be more difficult to define. In an attempt to better define this nebulous concept, Prinstein (2007) suggested that "the big three" for professional interviews are social skills, enthusiasm, and match. Applicants must therefore be appropriate, professional, and considerate (social skills), happy and energetic (enthusiasm), and have similar training and philosophy (match and fit) to the organization.

A key question is how the new colleague will fit into the existing interdisciplinary treatment team (Levendusky, 1986). There are certainly additional challenges in working with interdisciplinary teams, which may include working in a self-supporting manner, interacting with others who may not have high levels of mental health training, needing to be incredibly flexible, and losing touch with the core base of your psychological training (Humphrey & Kang, 2009). Talking about these topics during an on-site interview might provide you with some valuable insights about the working conditions in that particular professional setting. Moreover, asking questions about these topics may demonstrate to potential employers how perceptive you are in thinking about interactions with an interdisciplinary team.

There are several common errors that professional applicants make in emulating their academic counterparts: (a) talking in citations during an informal conversation, (b) demonstrating lack of confidence in a clinical setting by repeatedly mentioning the need to conduct more research, (c) demonstrating a lack of current therapeutic intervention knowledge involving drug regimens, and (d) continuously name-dropping training supervisors in an attempt to ride others' coattails (Levendusky, 1986). The professional on-site interview is, however, decidedly different from academic on-site interviews, especially when one is applying to a private practice. Barnett and Henshaw (2003) as well as Hodges and Connelly (2010) offered a sample of questions that you might ask when considering joining a private practice:

- Who owns the group, and who makes business decisions?
- How are referrals shared, and what assistance will be provided to help me get started?
- Who will my supervisor be? Who will my colleagues be?
- What administrative support is available?
- What are the specific components of the job?
- What percentage of the income I generate goes to the practice and what percentage to me?
- If I am interviewing for a vacancy, why did the last person leave?
- What if I decide to leave the practice: Can I take my patients with me?
- What benefits do I receive, such as malpractice insurance and continuing education? Is there a budget for supporting professional development?
- Am I allowed to decide which patients I will treat?
- What supervision and on-call coverage opportunities and obligations are there?

- What are the criteria for evaluation and how does one become an owner or partner?
- What are the unwritten rules (if any) that do not appear on the formal job description?

For the professional position interview, there may be a panel interview where multiple applicants are interviewed as a group (Crespi, Fischetti, & Lopez, 1998); these are sometimes called *open-house interviews* (Prinstein, 2007). There is also the possibility that an interview may be set up to occur at a regional or national conference using a prearranged placement service (Hodges & Connelly, 2010).

Illegal Questions, With Answering Strategies

Sometimes illegal or inappropriate questions are asked because of the ignorance of the interviewer, without the intent of harm. As Hodges and Connelly (2010) put it, "They *should* know better, but they don't always" (p. 70). There are two general principles at play here. First, potential employers may ask questions directly related to the job; these are known as *bona fide occupational qualifications* (DeLuca, 1997). Second, the goal of interviewing and hiring is to be able to select the person best suited for the job; in other words, to discriminate between qualified and unqualified applicants. This type of discrimination is appropriate and expected—but only using criteria that are bona fide occupational qualifications. It is illegal to discriminate on the basis of national origin, for example, because of Title VII of the Civil Rights Act of 1964 (DeLuca, 1997). Thus, questions such as "Where were you born?" or "What kind of accent am I detecting?" are illegal. Search committee members also cannot ask any question during an interview that relates to your race, religion, age, gender, or disability. In addition, in some states, inquiries about your sexual orientation are illegal as well. A list of legal and illegal questions is presented in Exhibit 7.5.

There are other types of questions that may not be technically illegal (depending on state and local laws) but are inappropriate—questions such as "Are you married?" "What is your maiden name?" or "How long have you been disabled?" Answers to these questions are not linked to bona fide occupational qualifications for either academic or professional positions with your doctorate in psychology. How do you handle these types of questions during your on-site interview? One of the ways to respond is to try to determine what concerns led the

EXHIBIT 7.5

Legal and Illegal Interview Questions

Identify which of the following questions should not be asked of you during an interview:
1. Where were you born?
2. What does your husband/wife do?
3. Are you authorized to work in the United States?
4. How tall are you?
5. What church do you attend?
6. Do you anticipate any absences from work on a regular basis?
7. What is your religion?
8. What is your race or ethnic origin?
9. When did you graduate from high school?
10. What is your maiden name?
11. Do you have any restrictions on your ability to travel?
12. Do you plan to have children?
13. How old are you?
14. Do you have a disability?
15. Are you able to perform the essential functions of this job with or without reasonable accommodations?
16. Are you a citizen of the United States?
17. Why are you in a wheelchair?
18. Are you over the age of 18?
19. Are there any organizations you belong to that you consider relevant to your ability to perform this job?
20. Are you married?
21. Do you have childcare arrangements?
22. With whom do you live?

(Items 3, 6, 11, 15, 18, 19 are all legal questions, the rest are not.)

potential employer to ask the question and address those rather than the literal questions you are asked:

> Inappropriate questions about partners and children often reflect employers' legitimate concerns about whether you will accept and keep a position. An employer who asks what your spouse or partner does is perhaps trying to figure out whether you will accept the job if it is offered, worrying that if you have a spouse, it might be harder to get you to take it. (Heiberger & Vick, 1999, para. 4)

A good response, then, is an indication that these concerns will not interfere with your job performance or likelihood of staying at the institution. Some authors have suggested using deflection methods (DeLuca, 1997; Hodges & Connelly, 2010), but questions that are more egregious may require additional actions, such as filing a local complaint with the Equal Employment Opportunity Commission. If, for example, you are in the midst of a job interview and you are asked,

"How old are you?" some possible responses could be the following, offered by Hodges and Connelly (2010):

- How does my age relate to the job?
- Why is that important to know?
- I don't think that the interview police allow that kind of question to be asked. [Humor intended.] Why do you want to know my age?

The last question is a nice way to let the interviewer know that they made a mistake and to allow him or her to retract the question gently. DeLuca (1997) recommended the following types of responses:

- Old enough to know I want to work here.
- Young enough to enjoy every day.

The Bottom Line: Top Recommendations for New Doctorates

You may not have much control over certain aspects of the on-site interview: the roster of individuals that you meet, the constituencies with whom you interact (e.g., community members, students), or even the choice of restaurant. However, one component you do have control over is the talk you may be asked to give in front of an interdisciplinary team and/or faculty and students. Our advice is to practice, practice, and practice. If you are talking about your dissertation, which is complete or nearly complete, you should not have to walk around with paper cues to remind you about the details. Practice your talk until you deliver it perfectly, and without notes. Make sure you practice in an environment that is similar to that of the real interview. For example, get dressed up, use a clicker to advance your slides, and take questions at the end. Have your practice audience members ask you questions that you might expect, but also have them ask some "curve ball" questions as well; it is better to practice your reactions with your friends and colleagues than to display them in the midst of your interview. If you do not know the answer, say so, but think about offering your expert opinion (being sure to label it as speculation). The entire process can be daunting, but the more you practice and prepare for what is expected, the more confidence you will have on those occasions where the unexpected occurs.

From the Trenches—Applicant Experiences and Advice

My worst job interview experience was being late for my job talk. First, no one told me about how I was supposed to get to campus after arriving at the airport (apparently there was miscommunication on their part about who was to convey this information to me). I assumed someone would pick me up (based on my prior job interview and interviews held at my doctoral institution), but after hearing nothing, I finally contacted the department 2 days before my interview to clarify how I would get from the airport to the college. They told me I was supposed to rent a car and drive myself, so I hurriedly made my reservation and got directions. Unfortunately, the department administrative assistant who scheduled my flight and prepared my itinerary did not give me enough time between when my flight landed and my first meeting. I was stuck in traffic (the airport was in a major city) and missed my first meeting and was 10 minutes late to my job talk. Fortunately, I still gave a great talk, but my stress levels were through the roof. To make matters worse, the administrative assistant also did not give me enough time to get from the college to the airport on the last day. The faculty realized this and made an effort to have my interview end 1 hour earlier, but despite this I still ended up missing my flight (which was the last one of the day). So, what advice do I have for those on the job market? Make sure you know all of the details for your interview ahead of time, and if you are worried about travel or time, talk to the department beforehand!

—PhD in social psychology, assistant professor
at a private university in the Midwest

Becoming a Great Candidate 8
The Preparation

Preparing to go on the job market begins much earlier than when you start writing your first cover letter. Although most candidates do not seriously start preparing for this process until they begin their dissertation or their clinical internship, to be competitive, the best time to start is toward the beginning of your doctoral or graduate career. The purpose of this early preparation is to establish a relevant record of accomplishments that are desirable to your future employer. Even if you are nearing the end of your graduate career and have not yet begun to think about this process, the suggestions in this chapter will help you discover what you have already done right and where you could focus your attention in the last year or two you have left. We also recommend that you consult resources such as Hammer and Yost Hammer (2009) and Sufka (2009) to assist in planning during your graduate education. These early investments can yield valuable returns in making the transition from doctoral training to first job. Exhibit 8.1 presents a timeline for preparing yourself for the job market during your graduate training.

If you have identified a range of job types that you are potentially interested in pursuing (i.e., academic or professional, including the types of jobs within those categories), your next step is to identify the types of experiences and skills that are required or desirable for those positions. Speaking

EXHIBIT 8.1

Timeline for Preparing Yourself to Be a Great Candidate

First year of your doctoral program
- Start building connections with faculty members who may be potential letter writers (you will need at least three, preferably four).
- Think about who might serve on your committee and start attending their lab meetings, if possible, to establish ongoing close relationships.
- Attend at least one professional conference, even if you are not presenting.
- Perform well in your courses—your instructors may be future letter writers.
- Be collegial and attend faculty social events.
- Try to get involved in a grant-funded project as a research assistant.
- Seek out a teaching assistant opportunity (even if you do not plan on procuring a teaching position when you graduate). Attend any training session or workshop available in your department or in your program. This can help you procure letters of recommendation, give you early teaching experience, and provide opportunities for people to give you feedback on your professional interactions with others.
- Try to identify a possible peer mentor—someone who is about 2 years ahead of you and has similar career goals (e.g., academic, clinical, industry).

Second year of your doctoral program
- Get a model of a curriculum vitae (CV) for any of the types of jobs you might want after graduating. Start seeking out opportunities that will help you fill in the appropriate sections.
- Become a student representative for a department or university committee and/or volunteer to help with departmental events to start accumulating service experience and to network with peers and faculty on campus.
- Be collegial and attend faculty social events.
- Pursue publishable research projects, especially if this is important for your future career goals in academia or research-oriented professional positions. Express interest in being involved in your advisor's work or current projects by, for example, helping with book chapters or presentations.
- Present at least one poster at a professional conference.
- Try to find a teaching assistantship, take a course on teaching, or attend workshops on teaching, especially if you are thinking of pursuing a career in academia or even a clinical position.
- Attend professional development workshops within your department or that are offered for all graduate students.

Third year of your doctoral program
- Try to write one manuscript for one of the projects you completed in your first 2 years.
- To provide new opportunities for publishing and presenting, begin new research projects or affiliate yourself with projects other faculty members are working on.
- Continue fostering relationships with professors to solidify letters of recommendation, even though you may not be taking classes anymore.
- For managerial experience, try to take on the role of supervising undergraduate research assistants or interns.
- Offer to help professors with journal reviews or letters of recommendation for undergraduate students with whom you have worked closely.
- If you are pursuing a career in academia or industry, try to get some experience writing a grant, either for an ongoing project or a new project.
- Develop a draft of your CV.
- Continue to seek teaching assistant and/or teaching-oriented professional development opportunities, especially if relevant to your future career goals.

EXHIBIT 8.1 (*Continued*)

- To improve your public speaking skills, present at least one paper at a professional conference.
- Think about becoming an informal mentor to a new graduate student.
- Take a professional development course or attend professional development workshops relevant to your career goals.
- If relevant to your career goals, begin compiling materials for a teaching portfolio by, for example, gathering student evaluations, sample syllabi, and course materials.

Fourth and fifth years of your doctoral program
- Add yourself to relevant Listservs and begin browsing job advertisements relevant to your career goals to note what types of positions are available and where they are located. Review job advertisements to see what application materials are required so you can be prepared with the appropriate supplemental documents.
- Keep connections with faculty other than your advisor through taking courses, attending other lab meetings, and meeting to discuss relevant ongoing research, teaching, internship, or professional activities.
- If research productivity is relevant to your career goals, work on establishing your own research lab with your own projects (rather than just working on those your advisor is overseeing). Supervise and mentor undergraduates as research assistants.
- Continue to focus on publishing your research, particularly if you are seeking an academic position or research-orientation professional position.
- If you are pursuing an academic position, seek teaching positions for which you are the instructor of record. This could include summer classes at your institution or even lecturer or adjunct positions at other local institutions (e.g., community colleges or other colleges or universities in the area).
- Seek opportunities to be a student reviewer for journals. This likely requires you to specifically ask faculty members to keep you in mind when they are asked to review a relevant article.
- Keep attending professional development workshops or job search programs offered at your university.
- If required for the types of positions you will be seeking when you graduate, draft your research and teaching statement. Continue updating and refining your CV.
- Talk with graduate students who have successfully obtained positions relevant to your career goals. Ask to sit in on and provide feedback for their practice job talks (especially if you are pursuing an academic or research-oriented professional position).
- Continue compiling materials for a teaching portfolio.

Last 12 months in the program
May–July
- Ask letter writers for letters (May–June).
- Seek out resources online, at your university career center, and from other people in your program to help you learn about the application materials and process.
- Draft main application documents (i.e., CV, cover letter, research statement, teaching statement).
- Seek feedback on main application documents from knowledgeable individuals.

August–September
- Start looking at relevant job postings. Academic institutions typically post advertisements starting in August through November, though some may be posted later if the positions become available because of retirements or the introduction of visiting assistant professor positions. Professional advertisements may be posted as early as August for positions starting a year later but may also appear as late as spring as well.

(*continued*)

EXHIBIT 8.1 (*Continued*)

- Prepare the materials you will be providing to letter writers. Give these materials to your letter writers about a month before your first letter is due.
- Begin to tailor your cover letters and documents to specific positions.
- Gather and summarize your teaching evaluations and assemble your teaching portfolio (if required).
- Order graduate transcripts to have on hand for the institutions or organizations that request them.
- Begin preparing your research talk (if required for the positions you are seeking).

October
- The first applications for faculty positions are often due October 1 (deadlines will typically extend until March 1). Have copies of reprints, transcripts, and envelopes ready to send out. Always review the materials in print before you mail them to make sure you have institution-specific information correct.
- Prepare answers to standard phone interview questions and seek feedback.
- Finalize your research talk and take as many opportunities as possible to practice it in front of faculty, peers, and lab groups (if relevant). Remember to practice talking informally about your research as well.
- Make preparations for short notice coverage of classes, meetings, or clients in case you have to leave town for interviews.
- Think about increasing your line of credit, if needed, to help cover the cost of interviews you have to pay for in advance and have reimbursed later.

November–March
- Stay on top of your deadlines. Your application should always arrive before the review begins date.
- Check to see that your application materials and letters of recommendation have been received.
- Keep alert for alternative job options, including postdoctoral fellowships, research and clinical fellowships, lecturer positions, visiting professor positions, and adjunct positions. Also keep in mind the variety of professional positions that are available.
- Continue to devote time to relevant projects (e.g., your dissertation) or duties (e.g., your clients) to ensure ongoing productivity or timely completion of your degree.

with faculty advisors, recent graduates, or people currently employed in the types of jobs you hope to get can help you gather information about the qualities and characteristics desired by various types of institutions or organizations. Be especially attuned to the potential need for postdoctoral experience for certain academic (e.g., research-oriented clinical psychology positions) or industry career paths (Schwebel & Karver, 2004; Z. Smith & Sutton-Grier, 2010). Reviewing job advertisements will provide you not only with a better idea of what jobs are available but also what qualifications, emphases, skills, or even application materials, are required (Clifton & Buskist, 2005). This is particularly true for nonacademic positions where required skills and experiences are often specifically delineated. The documents required in application packages are discussed in Exhibit 8.2.

EXHIBIT 8.2

What the Literature Says . . . About Documents Required in Application Packages

The documents you include in your application are typically the only information a search committee has with which to evaluate you. In preparing to enter the job market, it is important to pursue experiences that can be positioned in these documents to make you a desirable candidate. Having a clear understanding of what documents are typically required can provide you with an understanding of the skills and experiences search committees are looking for. To help graduate students prepare for the academic job market, Clifton and Buskist (2005) analyzed over 1,200 job advertisements from a variety of academic institutions. Their analysis revealed that the majority of advertisements, regardless of the rank of the advertised position, requested a curriculum vitae, letters of recommendation, copies of article reprints, and a cover letter. Less than half the advertisements required applicants to include a research statement, teaching statement, or copies of graduate transcripts. Very few advertisements requested teaching evaluations, sample course syllabi, or teaching portfolios.

Item	% of times required
Vitae	96.4% (95.8% of assistant professor advertisements)
References	90.3% (95.3% of assistant professor advertisements)
Reprints	60.5% (68.1% of assistant professor advertisements)
Cover letter	59.6% (69.4% of assistant professor advertisements)
Research interests	38.8% (41.4% of assistant professor advertisements)
Teaching philosophy	25% (29.8% of assistant professor advertisements)
Graduate transcripts	14.5% (22.6% of assistant professor advertisements)
Evaluations	10.4% (22.8% of assistant professor advertisements)
Syllabi	0.7% (2.0% of assistant professor advertisements)
Teaching portfolio	0.6% (2.6% of assistant professor advertisements)

Seek Opportunities to Build Expertise

After identifying your vocational options and the expertise required for these positions, your next step is to seek opportunities to build up experiences that will make you an excellent job candidate. For any academic position, and for many professional positions, your goals will likely include establishing a record of research, teaching, and service. For clinical or counseling positions, your practicum and internship experience is also central to your job preparation. Keeping these areas in mind as you progress through your graduate education and any postdoctoral position will ensure that you have a well-rounded application package when you enter the job market. In addition to building experience and expertise in these areas, developing and maintaining positive relationships with your mentors, peers, and individuals outside your institution

From the Trenches—Employer Experiences and Advice

We look for a strong balance of teaching and research experience (we are a teaching institution that places a high value on professional development). If someone has completed a course of training related to the teaching of psychology or has involvement in STP [Society for Teaching Psychology] (APA Division 2), that moves the person to the "take a second look" pile.

—Linda W., PhD in peace psychology, professor, private university in the Midwest

will uniquely contribute to your attractiveness as a candidate. More information about each of these areas is reviewed later in this chapter.

There are several other opportunities you can seek out during your graduate and postdoctoral career that can help you become a better candidate. The following suggestions may provide you with a glimpse into the perspective of those who will be involved in critical aspects of your job search. It is likely that at some point during your graduate education, your present institution will be hiring. Typically, graduate students are invited (or sometimes required) to participate in this process. Attending other candidates' job talks can help you immeasurably in preparing for your own, both by giving you an understanding of the typical format, as well as by demonstrating what they do right (and wrong) and the types of questions that are asked following the talk. Graduate students may also be invited to participate in an informal meeting with candidates or in other informal social events or receptions. These too can be useful for you to attend and observe. Some institutions invite students to sit on hiring committees. Let your advisor know that you are interested in this opportunity and take advantage of the chance to review applications and see how hiring committees make their decisions. If you are pursuing a career in academia, seeing how the hiring process works from the inside will certainly prove enlightening.

In addition to participating on the other side of the hiring process, it can also be helpful to get the opportunity to cowrite letters of recommendation for undergraduate students. This gives you the chance to experience what you appreciate (and do not appreciate) when you are providing this service to others. A little introspection can help you prepare for interacting in the most useful way with your letter writers. Being a reviewer for conferences and journals (often facilitated by your advisor or another faculty member) can also help you gain a different perspective on this process and will likely help you in your future conference and manuscript submissions. Gaining these experiences typically requires that you let faculty know you are interested in all these opportunities so that they can facilitate these experiences for you. It would also be valu-

---

From the Trenches—Applicant Experiences and Advice

I worked for 5 years at our teaching center during my graduate studies, and was involved in both department- and university-level initiatives and projects. Understanding some of the key pressures that higher education is facing was a really asset for me.

—Sarah B., PhD in psychology, assistant professor at a liberal arts college in the Midwest

---

able to think about this process from the perspective of the departmental chairperson, as well as what it means to be a good departmental citizen. For excellent advice and insights about departmental citizenship (i.e., service, conscientiousness, and collegiality), see R. A. Smith (2009).

BUILDING A COHESIVE LINE OF RESEARCH

Although your graduate education is likely geared toward preparing you to be an independent and productive researcher, it may not always provide you with the best evidence of your success as a researcher. Publications in peer-reviewed journals, presentations of papers at professional conferences, and experience working on grant proposals are the best methods of establishing a record in research. It is important to begin your publication history during graduate school, and this takes planning.

Presenting papers, posters, or abstracts at local, regional, national, and international conferences during graduate school and postdoctoral training is an excellent way to enhance your research record. Attending conferences not only allows you to practice speaking about your research but also provides you with the opportunity to get to know people in your field. For example, Sego and Richards (1995) suggested that "even if you have a couple of years before you start searching for your job, people who take interest in papers you present at professional conferences may watch your progress with an eye toward hiring you" (p. 2).

There are often many potential opportunities for creating publishable papers throughout your graduate career. Sowers-Hoag and Harrison (1998) advised that "every paper written and every professional work effort throughout your doctoral program should be considered a possible publication opportunity" (p. 14). This includes papers you write for courses you take, work you do for required research projects, and master's theses. Papers can also be written about small or preliminary research projects you undertake in the middle of your program in preparation for your dissertation. Although not usually enough evidence of research ability on their own, graduate research assistantships can also be valuable because they provide you with the opportunity to work with an established researcher, and you will likely receive valuable experience and opportunities to publish (Ginorio, Yee, Banks, & Todd-Bazemore, 2011).

Especially if you are interested in working at a research-oriented institution, getting experience with grant writing is an excellent way to enhance your qualifications and expertise. Whether you seek your own dissertation grants or work with faculty members on their grants, grant writing can provide you with excellent experience and confidence for obtaining external funding in the future. If you can get experience helping your mentor or another faculty member to locate possible sources of funding, write grant proposals, or work on funded projects, you can gain experience with the various stages of the grant process (Bem, 2004; Sternberg, 2004). It can also be helpful to start constructing your research statement midway through your graduate career. Writing a research plan forces you to think ahead and facilitates your ability to establish an independent line of research during your graduate career (J. Austin, 2002). If you have already started to think about your own program of research, writing a research statement will ensure you stay on track and refine your plans accordingly. It might also help you think about future publications that you can aim to have under review or published by the time you are applying for jobs. Furthermore, taking the time to think about your research as "programmatic" will likely help you build a more cohesive and unified line of research.

Another way you can get excellent experience is to start up your own research lab. J. Austin (2002) suggested the following:

> Talk to your adviser about carving out your own research niche within the larger research effort, where you do work motivated by your own original ideas on something related but oblique to what your adviser is doing in the rest of the lab. (para. 48)

A successful independent project (and potential resulting paper presentations or publications) can convince a committee that you are capable of independent research and can also provide you with the experience and confidence to speak about your future as an academic researcher. Furthermore, running your own research lab will give you the opportunity to supervise undergraduate research assistants, which can help you think about the ways you mentor, advise, and supervise undergraduates (and later, graduate students) with regard to your research.

GAINING TEACHING EXPERIENCE AND EXPERTISE

It is important that you seek out teaching opportunities and spend time in the classroom during your graduate and postdoctoral experiences (Ginorio et al., 2011). If you are not automatically offered teaching assistant positions or if you have secured other funding that makes it unnecessary for you obtain these positions, try to find a position anyway. You may be required to find one in another department if you already have funding. However, this may be beneficial because you should have teaching assistant experience in a broad array of classes before you graduate. It is also important that you are the instructor of record for at least one, if not two or three classes, before you graduate. It is helpful if these classes include an introductory level course as well as an upper division or specialty class in your research area. If these opportunities are not available to you during the academic year at your institution, it might be possible for you to teach a summer course or a course at an area community college. Last, take advantage of any and all formal training for teaching assistants offered through your department or university. This can include one-time training sessions or workshops, participating in ongoing teaching and learning communities, or even enrolling in graduate classes that teach you how to teach. If formal training is not offered, you can also engage in more informal training by observing good faculty role models from your department teach in their classrooms, as well as by requesting faculty or peers to observe and critique your teaching. Even if you do not anticipate pursuing a career that includes teaching, you can gain broadly applicable skills through these experiences.

In addition to recording your teaching assistantships, instructor positions, and training or courses on teaching, you should also keep track of the student, peer, or faculty evaluations you procure from these experiences. As described in Chapter 4, many academic institutions will ask you for "evidence of teaching excellence," which often means the committee would like formal evaluations of your teaching. Your university will typically gather course evaluations using a standardized tool; the results of these measures, including accompanying student comments, can serve as evidence of teaching excellence. Other materials may also serve you well in presenting a teaching portfolio. It is important to keep track of all these documents as you teach. Chapter 4 provides ideas for what types of materials would be useful to save.

From the Trenches—Employer Experiences and Advice

Gain as much experience as you can teaching a range of courses as well as developing professional activities (e.g., publications, presentations) so that you look good on paper. Get involved in professional organizations and network so that your letters can come from professionals beyond your immediate professors.

—Linda W., PhD in peace and political psychology, professor of psychology and international human rights at a private university in the Midwest

ESTABLISHING A RECORD OF SERVICE

Although it is not necessarily central to your application, showing that you are willing to get involved and to engage with the needs of the department would be valuable to a potential colleague in or outside of academia (see R. A. Smith, 2009). Serving as a student representative on committees, helping to organize social events or activities, or becoming involved in a graduate student organization are all ways to increase your service activities. Furthermore, serving on hiring committees, working on letters of recommendation for undergraduate students, and being a reviewer for professional journals and conferences with your advisor or other faculty members will both count as service and provide you with useful perspectives on job-related evaluations you will undergo. If you are involved in community service outside your institution, keep track of those activities as well because they may be viewed as signs of a good citizen to search committees and may involve activities or skills that could be highlighted on your application for professional positions.

SUPPLEMENTAL ACTIVITIES FOR PROFESSIONAL POSITIONS

Engaging in these activities (i.e., research, teaching, and service) is relevant to applying for professional positions as well, even if the type of job you are seeking will not require you to focus primarily on research, teaching, or service activities. Employers typically hire individuals with PhDs because they have expertise in a particular field and/or because they have research skills that will be useful to the organization. As such, an extensive history of research experience will make you a stronger candidate for most professional positions. As a graduate student, your research activities were likely collaborative and involved management and delegation to research assistants; these are valued skills to many professional employers. Teaching experience signifies that you are able to present material in an organized and coherent manner, a useful skill when you are making presentations to clients either to secure a contract or deliver the final product. Service also typically involves committee work, which indicates your ability to work well with others and suggesting collegiality.

If you are aware of your interest in pursuing consulting, marketing, or government positions early in your graduate career, it would be beneficial to pursue job opportunities, internship, or volunteer opportunities in those fields while you are still in graduate school (Mielcarek & Borbely, 2011). These could be pursued as part-time or summer positions and would not only make you a better candidate when you graduate but would also help you determine whether that particular career direction is appropriate for you and allow you to start building the specific skills you will need to be successful in that line of work. Clinical and counseling practicums and internships that are built into graduate programs in these areas serve a similar purpose: to provide you with opportunities to work in several different settings with different populations to hone your interests and skills (in addition to providing you with the opportunity to accumulate some of the hours necessary for licensing purposes).

BUILDING STRONG RELATIONSHIPS AND NETWORKS

Your primary relationship and resource during your graduate (or postdoctoral) career will be your advisor (or supervisor). Maintaining a good relationship is paramount in getting the support that will help you prepare for a successful career, beyond simply a good recommendation. Whatever you can do to foster a productive, open relationship with your advisor or supervisor should serve you well. However, these relationships do not always progress smoothly nor can any one individual offer you the perspectives you will likely need regarding all aspects of your job search. Getting to know other faculty members in your department and other relevant departments will also benefit you. Remember that even though you will be picking specific people to officially recommend you for a position, potential employers might also seek information about you from other people with whom they have established relationships (and who know you; Graduate College Career Services Office, University of Illinois Urbana–Champaign, 2006).

Collaboration with peers is also an invaluable networking opportunity. Peers not only offer great resources regarding job applications and search advice but they also tend to have excellent insights about building strong research and teaching records. Because you and your peers are likely all preparing to be hired following graduation, you should have similar goals to publish, present, gain teaching experience, and seek opportunities for service. Although there may be an element of competition among graduate students, it is unlikely that you will be competing for similar positions. As such, it is in your interest to engage in mutually beneficial collaborations on research and to share information and resources.

In addition to building strong relationships with faculty and graduate students at your institution, seeking connections outside your institution often becomes useful during the job search process. Becoming involved in your discipline's preeminent professional organization(s) and in the subsidiary divisions that represent your career interests can help you gather more information about those careers as well as offer networking opportunities. When you attend conferences, take advantage of opportunities for meeting people who may be your future colleagues or collaborators; these opportunities could occur during discussions following others' presentations or when following up with interested parties after your own presentations. Remember to be professional at all times in your personal presentation in these contexts. Beyond making contacts for potential future employment, building a network of colleagues who are familiar with you and your work will enhance your research productivity and intellectual resources. Participation in electronic discussion lists, blogs, or professional forums can also connect you with a large group of individuals with similar interests and may culminate in collaborative presentations, grants, and papers. Furthermore, if you are actively engaged in research with other scholars, it will be easier for you to identify as a colleague than as a student.

Another important consideration is managing your online presence, or electronic persona. Most individuals are represented online in one or more settings, including perhaps a listing of your name, research interests, and contact information on your graduate department's website; a profile you set up on a professional networking website such as LinkedIn; or a professional website that you maintain. Of course, you likely also have a more personal or social presence online as well, including a personal blog, a personal website, a twitter account, and profiles on Facebook or other social networking websites that may have varying levels of privacy settings. Keep in mind that family or friends may have posted information about you or tagged you in pictures on their personal profiles, blogs, or websites as well. Furthermore, it is also possible that organizations with which you are affiliated (e.g., religious groups, athletic groups, advocacy groups, social groups, or other groups you volunteer for) have listed you as a member or have posted articles or newsletters that feature you. Last, there may also be someone who has the same first and last name as you and who has posted scandalous information and pictures online.

With the variety of ways it is possible for potential employers to access information about you (or someone they think is you), it is essential that you Google yourself before you begin applying for jobs. It is likely that your potential employer will, once they are considering you as a finalist for their position (SkillStorm, 2009). Any management of online information about you should occur before you send out applications, and, given the difficulty of permanently removing pictures or information online, you may want to consider carefully what you post online well before you actually enter the job market.

The Waiting Game

Spending years preparing to put together the best application package you can for your perfect job after earning your doctorate is a challenging process. Once you send out your applications, you get to sit back and enjoy the fruits of your labor, right? Unfortunately, anyone who has gone through the process will tell you that the intermediary period between sending out applications and waiting to be contacted for screening interviews, on-campus interviews, and the elusive job offer is one of the most stressful parts of this process. In Chapters 6 and 7, we said that you should be ready to receive an invitation for screening interviews with as little notice as 2 to 3 days, and with a week or two for on-site interviews. Thus, you should prepare for these as much as possible before and after submitting your applications. However, you should also be prepared to engage in the inevitable last minute planning required for each of these types of interviews.

The other stressful aspect of the postapplication period is not knowing whether your application was received and whether all your materials arrived on time. One of the benefits of online application systems is that you can find out whether your application package is complete and whether your letters of recommendation were received. Employers do not keep applicants apprised of their review process, so you will not know whether the business or institution typically conducts screening (or phone) interviews, how many people they will be interviewing, or when interviews will take place.

Although you should always aim for your application materials to be received by (or before) the deadline, the search committee may not actually begin reviewing them for a week or two after that, and it can take weeks or even months before the first interview requests are made. As a result, you may apply for a position in early October and not hear from the search committee until late January, even if you are a top finalist for their position. Conversely, a position you applied for in early October may be filled by late November, but rejection letters may not be sent out until February, if at all. Furthermore, even if you do participate in an off-site interview in early November, and the search committee tells you they will contact you in 2 weeks about the possibility of an on-site interview, it is possible you will not hear from them again; however, they may also contact you 2 months later to invite you for an on-site interview and follow up with a job offer.

These delays can be due to a number of different factors, including delays in scheduling meetings, references that take longer to contact than expected, and delays at human resources or another administrative department (e.g., inviting a candidate to the campus likely involves approval from a dean, provost, and vice-president or president). There could also be funding issues that delay offers or invitations to interviews. Last, it is possible that you were not a top candidate but became so after the top candidates were interviewed and rejected (or after they turned down the job offer). At the job offer stage, the likely interval between an on-site interview and a job offer is about 2 weeks (and

---

From the Trenches—Applicant Experiences and Advice

I honestly think that I was pretty well prepared for the job search because I had a terrific advisor who kept me on track. The one thing I would change is that I had prepared these materials over the summer and received feedback from my advisor before fall semester started. Several deadlines for jobs are in September, and I know that I sent out a handful of applications that were not polished because I had yet to receive feedback from my advisor. You should also plan on giving your advisor and other references plenty of time prior to any deadlines.

—Kimberly M., PhD in social psychology, assistant professor at a public university in the West

---

often longer). Search committees often optimistically underestimate timeframes, which can be stressful if the anticipated date of notification passes with no contact from them. It is also possible that an offer was made to another candidate who is involved in negotiations with the company or institution. If the offer is declined, you may be next on the list. As you are waiting, keep your search active and continuing pursuing other options, even if you anticipate the offer.

The variability in the timeline of the postapplication process and the lack of communication from employers are especially stressful for applicants. Search committees rarely make timely efforts to tell rejected applicants at any stage that they did not get the job; however, not hearing from the search committee could mean that an administrative delay occurred or that that process was otherwise interrupted. To address this issue in the academic job market, a website has been created that is maintained and updated by applicants when they are contacted for off-site and on-site interviews or offered a position (http://psychjobsearch. wikidot.com). Personal connections can also be used to check the status of the process, but these should be used respectfully and sparingly.

The Bottom Line: Top Recommendations for New Doctorates

Regardless of the type of career you are pursuing, excelling in your graduate program will help you secure a desirable job after graduation. It is helpful to start building a record of experiences directly relevant to your chosen career path as early as possible; this will likely require you to be proactive and seek out opportunities throughout the duration of your program. For many positions in and outside of academia, establishing a strong record of research, teaching, and service will prepare you to be a good candidate and lead to a successful career. For research positions, find opportunities to present and publish papers as well as to apply for and secure grants. For teaching positions, you should have experience as a teaching assistant or an instructor of record for your own course, in addition to more informal supervisory experiences. Service can take many forms and can be completed through your department, your university, or the community. Experience in each of these areas will help you build skills and provide you with evidence of your success to share in your applications and interview. Equally important, this will help you develop and maintain connections with faculty and peers that can lead to letters of recommendation and future collaborations.

Appendix: Negotiating and Deciding Among Multiple Offers

Success! All of the preparation finally paid off, and you have received a job offer. Your hard work is about to culminate in gainful employment. It is typical to first receive news of an offer over the phone or through e-mail, with a written contract to follow. Even though your initial reaction might be to immediately accept the offer, you are not expected to do so over the phone. Instead, express your enthusiasm and gratitude, and avoid making a commitment to the position. The foremost goal of this phone call from the perspective of the employer is to reassess your interest in the position and preliminarily offer it to you. They will likely provide you with basic information about the offer, but specific details will follow in a second phone call, e-mail, or written contract. During one of your initial conversations they will also provide you with a timeline for making your decision (usually a few days or up to 2 weeks).[1]

---

[1]If you know that you are going to reject an offer, it is considerate to indicate this as soon as possible. A decision sooner rather than later benefits the organization because they can then offer the position to the next eligible candidate. It also benefits others who applied for the job, because you have removed yourself from the competition. Delaying your decision can leave the organization in a predicament and is unfair to the other applicants.

Negotiating the Offer

Negotiations can begin during your job interview and only end when you sign the contract. Negotiating is important not only because it could provide you with greater lifelong monetary compensation or other benefits but also because an unfavorable outcome to a negotiation has been associated with the belief that one is unfairly compensated for the contributions to the organization or institution (Porter, Conlon, & Barber, 2004). If you feel uncomfortable with negotiating, consider Vick and Heiberger's (2002) advice to job candidates to "present yourself as a colleague who is looking for what it takes to do the best job possible" (para. 15).

How typical is (successful) negotiating? In a study of 306 faculty members affiliated with school psychology graduate programs in the United States, Crothers et al. (2010) found that 65% of female and 68% of male faculty members negotiated for salary when hired or at a later point in their position. Of those who did negotiate, 74% of women and 85% of men reported a successful increase in their salary. Another study of a sample of 149 newly hired employees (half in industry and half in tenure-track faculty positions) found that the 74% of the sample who chose to negotiate increased their starting salaries by an average of $5,000 and that the amount gained through negotiation did not differ between those in academic versus industry positions (Marks & Harold, 2011).

Although negotiation is fairly common and expected both within and outside of academia, entering into negotiation is more likely to be fruitful under one (or both) of the following circumstances. First, you will have more leverage if you have competing offers. Not only might this provide you with added confidence to ask for what you want but might also present a good reason for an organization or institution to consider making your offer more enticing. The other scenario that offers you a sturdy platform for negotiating is if you are aware that the salary you are being offered is not commensurate with the "going rate." In other words, if after researching what individuals earn in similar positions with your potential employer and other employers, you determine that your offer is less than what others earn, you may have additional grounds for negotiation. Organizations such as the College and University Professional Association for Human Resources track salaries for faculty members in a variety disciplines throughout the United States (see http://www.cupahr. org/). Salary information for academic and professional psychologists is also widely available through the American Psychological Association (APA) Center for Workforce Studies (http://www.apa.org/workforce/about/index.aspx).

Whether or not you have salary statistics, a competing offer, or simply a desire for higher pay, it is important to be professional throughout the negotiation process. You are negotiating for the foundation of a career, and this process can set the tone for future relationships with your future supervisors. In addition, engaging in a cooperative rather than an antagonistic conversation can have a positive impact on you as well as on your future employer. For example, Marks and Harold (2011) reported that people felt better about their negotiated outcomes when they used collaborative approaches that actively considered both parties' concerns. Bradley (2001) explained that "you can look after your own interests and still make a good impression if you are firm (not rigid), assertive (not combative), and maintain high (not impossible) expectations" (para. 26).

The exact process of negotiation will be unique and will depend on a multitude of factors. Nonetheless, there are some basic "best practices" for negotiation in any field. Your first goal is to gather information about the offer and position itself. For example, find out about salary and other benefits included in the offer package. Second, once you have determined what they are offering you, it is your responsibility to find out how your offer compares with other people's offer packages. Is your salary competitive? Are your benefits reasonable? What "perks" are you being offered, and how do they stack up with what previous employees received? Be sure to look both within and outside of your potential place of employment for this information. Third, it is important that as you enter into the negotiation phase you have a straightforward, concise, and complete list of requests. Use your prior research into typical job offer packages to help construct the list. Everything should be requested in one or two sittings. The list should be prioritized and include only your most pressing requests. In creating this list, it is important for you to not only decide what you want but also what requests you are willing to relinquish. Last, as you move through the process, it is also important to be flexible. For example, if they cannot meet your salary needs, will they give you a signing bonus or more start-up money? It can be helpful to focus on the total package rather than on just one or two points.

One of the most common negotiating points is salary. Here, it is essential that you do your research on salary ranges for your field. Nowviskie (2010) recommended that you "do not discuss compensation without being informed as to what's equitable within the institution" (para. 8). Your goal is to find out whether what they are offering you is fair (on the basis of experience, education, and location). Most salary figures from publicly funded schools and entities are published. If these data are not available to you, you can find out what people in similar positions are making elsewhere. There are several resources for this type of information. The APA produces an annual salary report, as does the American Association of University Professors. The Bureau of Labor Statistics also has extensive information on salaries and benefits broken down by industry and region. Several other websites that could prove useful include WetFeet (http://www.wetfeet.com), Salary.com (http://www.salary.com), and JobStar Central (http://www.jobstar.org). As you find out typical salaries in other regions, recognize that there is great geographic variation in the cost of living. There are a number of online calculators to help you make appropriate adjustments. You might also consider contacting a current employee who was especially friendly during your interview and ask whether they would be comfortable sharing their salary range.

Once you have determined an appropriate estimated salary range, your negotiations should aim for the top of this range. However, be prepared to accept less. Many large employers have formal pay structures or set entry-level salaries at fixed levels and are therefore unable to negotiate. Sinclair (2006) described internal and external factors that contribute to an academic institution's ability to meet negotiation demands from new faculty; these include the university's available resources, the administration's desire to maintain internal equity, and the going salary rate for that rank and discipline among peer institutions in similar regions.

There are aspects of a job offer to negotiate other than salary. A common point of negotiation is compensation for moving expenses. This could include expenses for travel ahead of time to find a place to live, hotel expenses until you are settled, and reimbursement for movers and moving supplies. Some employers will have flexibility in their moving expense policy, whereas others may have rigid regulations about how much they will cover. Another common point of negotiation is the length of time you are given to decide on the offer. You may have an offer from an organization or institution that is not your first choice and you will thus need time to contact more preferable options to ascertain the likelihood that you will be considered seriously for positions in their organizations. Perhaps you anticipate another offer and want to use it as leverage for negotiation. Under either of these circumstances, it is reasonable to request an extension, but it is important to recognize that not all employers will readily grant you one, because they may have enticing back-up candidates who may not be available if they wait too long to make an offer. Other potential points of negotiation in academic and professional positions are listed in the Exhibit 1. A few studies examined the effect of gender on salary negotiation outcomes and found that women are less likely to negotiate (Babcock, Gelfand, Small, & Stayn, 2006) and that men receive larger salary negotiation payoffs (Gerhart & Rynes, 1991). Indeed, in the Crothers et al., (2010) study, among faculty members employed between 0 and 5 years, male faculty members earned on average $4,272 more than their female counterparts. One explanation for women's reluctance to negotiate is that it may result in negative responses from their future employer. For example, college

---

EXHIBIT 1

Negotiation Points in Academic and Professional Positions

Academic	Professional
▪ Salary	▪ Salary
▪ Start-up money	▪ Rank
▪ Teaching load or schedule	▪ Reporting date
▪ Rank	▪ Promotion schedule
▪ Years toward tenure	▪ Appraisal reviews
▪ Class assignments	▪ Signing bonus
▪ Travel support	▪ Time off (sick and paid)
▪ Research lab or office space	▪ Moving expenses
▪ Laboratory equipment	▪ Terms of employment
▪ Moving expenses	▪ Retirement (pension or employer contributions)
▪ Sabbatical options	▪ Medical, life, and disability insurance
▪ Graduate research assistants	▪ Stock purchase or savings plan
▪ Employment for a partner or spouse	▪ Professional development support
▪ Grants for summer research	
▪ Payment for membership to professional organizations	
▪ Research software	

students evaluated female candidates more negatively in their ability to initiate negotiations than they did male candidates (Bowles, Babcock, & Lai, 2007). However, research outcomes have indicated that gender differences in negotiation may be mitigated within social contexts that provide opportunities for negotiation (Small et al., 2007).

Handling Multiple Offers

Deciding between multiple job offers is a daunting task, but remember not to overlook the very positive reality that you have two (or more!) job offers. In other words, this is a good problem to have. When approaching this important decision, we strongly suggest that you gather as much information as possible. This information should include the details of the offer packages from both potential employers as well as pertinent information about the position itself that may or may not have been covered during your interview. This information can be used to evaluate all job offers, recognizing that each individual will place different weight on different aspects of the job (e.g., salary vs. promotion timeline, commute vs. health insurance).

Pertinent information about the position may vary based on whether or not you have been offered an academic or professional job. In academia,

---

EXHIBIT 2

Seven Factors in Evaluating Job Offers

- Nature of the work: Am I proud of the products or services of the employer? Is the job interesting to me? Does this position fit into my long-range career plans and personal goals?
- Your boss: Can I work with and get along with this person? You should feel comfortable with his or her interpersonal and management style. Your supervisor should be capable and interested in your growth.
- Salary and benefits: Is the salary at market level? Would taking this position create economic hardship? Do salary reviews and promotions occur on a regular basis? Think also of the benefits package when considering the offer.
- Your coworkers: Will I fit into the corporate culture?
- Typical work week: What is a typical workweek like? How many hours a week does the position require?
- Location: Do you like the location or region where you'll be working and living? How long and arduous is the commute?
- Organizational flexibility: Is the organization rigid? Does it work by strict rules? Will the employer be flexible during emergencies? How will this position alter my lifestyle? If it will, can I handle such changes?

Note. Data from Skidmore College Career Services (2011).

you may want to find out about your teaching load; the expected balance of teaching, research, and service; the courses you would teach and how that is decided; as well as tenure and promotion policies. For professional positions, pertinent information could include questions about your job duties, expectations for travel, training schedule, work culture, and company stability (see Exhibit 2).

Accepting an Offer

Whether you are juggling several offers or negotiating with just one potential employer, it is important that you continue your job search until you have received and signed the official offer. It is possible that funding will be revoked or decisions reversed during the negotiation period, which means you should not notify other organizations or institutions that you are withdrawing your application until you have secured the position in writing. Once you do have the offer and return the written letter, let your advisors, references, and other departments actively considering you for a position know that you have accepted a job. If this includes rejecting another active offer, be gracious and prompt—remember, others are waiting too. Then, after sending letters of appreciation to your advisers and references, it is time to celebrate!

References

American Psychological Association. (2009). Psychologist and professor are among the country's hottest jobs. *Monitor on Psychology, 40*(11), 11.

American Psychological Association. (2011). Preparing future faculty. *American Psychological Association.* Retrieved from http://www.apa.org/education/grad/future-faculty.aspx

Argow, B., & Beane, R. (2009). Developing your research statement. *On the Cutting Edge.* Retrieved from http://serc.carleton.edu/NAGTWorkshops/careerprep/jobsearch/research_statement.html

Armstrong, P., Stanton, K., & Mannheimer, K. L. (2005, June 22). How would you teach this class? *The Chronicle of Higher Education.* Retrieved from http://chronicle.com/article/How-Would-You-Teach-This-Cl/45011/

Austin, J. (2002, July 26). Writing a research statement. *Science Careers.* Retrieved from http://sciencecareers.sciencemag.org/career_development/previous_issues/articles/1820/writing_a_research_plan

Austin, R. N. (2006, April 14). Writing the teaching statement. *Science Careers.* Retrieved from http://sciencecareers.sciencemag.org/career_magazine/previous_issues/articles/2006_04_14/writing_the_teaching_statement

Babcock, L., Gelfand, M., Small, D., & Stayn, H. (2006). Gender differences in the propensity to initiate negotiations. In D. De Cremer, M. Zeelenberg, & J. K. Murnighan (Eds.), *Social psychology and economics* (pp. 239–262). Mahwah, NJ: Erlbaum.

Barnett, J. E., & Henshaw, E. (2003). Training to begin a private practice. In M. J. Prinstein & M. D. Patterson (Eds.), *The portable mentor: Expert guide to a successful career in psychology* (pp. 145–156). New York, NY: Kluwer Academic.

Baron, D. (2001, December 21). To whom it may concern: Reading job applications. *The Chronicle of Higher Education*. Retrieved from http://chronicle.com/article/To-Whom-It-May-Concern-/45527/

Basalla, S., & Debelius, M. (2007). *"So what are you going to do with that?" Finding careers outside academia*. Chicago, IL: University of Chicago Press.

Beatty, J. E., Leigh, J. S. A., & Dean, K. L. (2009). Finding our roots: An exercise for creating a personal teaching philosophy statement. *Journal of Management Education, 33*, 115–130. doi:10.1177/1052562907310642

Bem, D. J. (2004). Writing the empirical journal article. In J. M. Darley, M. P. Zanna, & H. L. Roediger, III, (Eds.), *The compleat academic: A career guide* (2nd ed., pp. 185–219). Washington, DC: American Psychological Association.

Benson, T. A., & Buskist, W. (2005). Understanding "excellence in teaching" as assessed by psychology faculty search committees. *Teaching of Psychology, 32*, 47–49. doi:10.1207/s15328023top3201_11

Bock, K. (2005, October 28). Common job-hunting blunders. *The Chronicle of Higher Education*. Retrieved from http://chronicle.com/article/Common-Job-Hunting-Blunders/44953/

Bowles, H., Babcock, L., & Lai, L. (2007). Social incentives for gender differences in the propensity to initiate negotiations: Sometimes it does hurt to ask. *Organizational Behavior and Human Decision Processes, 103*, 84–103. doi:10.1016/j.obhdp.2006.09.001

Bradley, G. (2000, September 15). Careers for Ph.D.'s in the nonprofit world. *The Chronicle of Higher Education*. Retrieved from http://chronicle.com/article/Careers-For-PhD-s-in-the/46376

Bradley, G. (2001, October 8). Negotiating salary in the nonacademic world. *The Chronicle of Higher Education*. Retrieved from http://chronicle.com/article/Negotiating-Salary-in-the/45407/

Brems, C., Lampman, C., & Johnson, M. E. (1995). Preparation of applications for academic positions in psychology. *American Psychologist, 50*, 533–537. doi:10.1037/0003-066X.50.7.533

Brown, C. S. (2009). Negotiating the application and interview process. In S. F. Davis, P. J. Giordano, & C. A. Licht (Eds.), *Your career in psychology: Putting your graduate degree to work* (pp. 59–73). Malden, MA: Wiley-Blackwell.

Burns, R. G., & Kinkade, P. (2008). Finding fit: The nature of a successful faculty employment search in criminal justice. *Journal of Criminal Justice, 36,* 372–378. doi:10.1016/j.jcrimjus.2008.06.005

Campbell, R. W., Horner-Devine, M. C., Lartigue, J., & Rollwagen Bollens, G. C. (2001). Preparing for an academic job interview: Frequently asked questions for on-site and phone interviews. *Dissertations Initiative for the Advancement of Climate Change Research.* Retrieved from http://disccrs.org/sites/default/files/interviewhints.pdf

Campbell, S. (2010, June 21). Salary history and salary requirements. *1st-Writer.com.* Retrieved from http://www.1st-writer.com/Salary.htm

Caplan, P. J. (1993). *Lifting a ton of feathers: A woman's guide for surviving in the academic world.* Toronto, Canada: University of Toronto Press.

Career Advising and Planning Services. (2010). *Interviewing for research and teachings appointments: A resource guide for doctoral students, PhDs, and post-docs on the academic job market.* Retrieved from https://caps.uchicago.edu/resourcecenter/handouts/Interviewing%20for%20Academic%20Appointments-2010%20rev.pdf

Career Services, University of Pennsylvania. (n.d.). *Writing an effective research statement.* Retrieved from http://www.vpul.upenn.edu/careerservices/gradstud/samples/Writing_Research_Statement.ppt

Chin, E. M. (2000). Using externships, internships, and postdoctoral placements to your advantage. In S. F. Davis, P. J. Giordano, & C. A. Licht (Eds.), *Your career in psychology: Putting your graduate degree to work* (pp. 135–150). Malden, MA: Wiley-Blackwell.

Clifton, J., & Buskist, W. (2005). Preparing graduate students for academic position in psychology: Suggestions from job advertisements. *Teaching of Psychology, 32,* 265–267.

Cook, C. E., Kaplan, M., Nidiffer, J. N., & Wright, M. C. (2001, November). Preparing future faculty—faster. *AAHE Bulletin, 54*(3), 3–7.

Crespi, T. D., Fischetti, B. A., & Lopez, P. G. (1998). Supervision and mentoring for professional employment. *School Psychology International, 19,* 239–250. doi:10.1177/0143034398193004

Crosby, O. (1999, Summer). Resumes, applications, and cover letters. *Occupational Outlook Quarterly, 43*(2), 18–29.

Crossman, E. K., & Nazzaro, J. R. (1976). The vita. In P. J. Woods, (ed.), *Career opportunities for psychologists* (pp.53–61). Washington, DC: American Psychological Association.

Crothers, L. M., Hughes, T. L., Schmitt, A. J., Theodore, L. A., Lipinski, J., Bloomquist, A. J., & Altman, C. L. (2010). Has equity been achieved? Salary and promotion negotiation practices of a national sample of school psychology university faculty. *The Psychologist-Manager Journal, 13,* 40–59. doi:10.1080/10887150903553790

Darley, J. M., & Zanna, M. P. (2004). The hiring process in academia. In J. M. Darley, M. P. Zanna, & H. L. Roediger, III, (Eds.), *The compleat academic: A career guide* (2nd ed., pp. 31–56). Washington, DC: American Psychological Association.

Darley, J. M., Zanna, M. P., & Roediger, H. L., III. (Eds). (2004). *The compleat academic: A career guide* (2nd ed.). Washington, DC: American Psychological Association.

Delph, L. F. (2010, October 6). Rules for science job talks. *Inside Higher Ed.* Retrieved from http://www.insidehighered.com/advice/2010/10/06/delph

DeLuca, M. J. (1997). *Best answers to the 201 most frequently asked interview questions.* New York, NY: McGraw-Hill.

Durand, A.-P. (2011, March 11). Keys to the cover letter. *Inside Higher Ed.* Retrieved from http://www.insidehighered.com/advice/2011/03/11/advice_on_the_cover_letter_for_academic_jobs

Edgerton, R., Hutchings, P., & Quinlan, K. (1991). *The teaching portfolio: Capturing the scholarship in teaching.* Washington, DC: The American Association for Higher Education.

Ernst, M. (2002). *Requesting a letter of recommendation.* Retrieved from http://www.cs.washington.edu/homes/mernst/advice/request-recommendation.html

Feldman, D. B., & Silvia, P. J. (2010). *Public speaking for psychologists.* Washington, DC: American Psychological Association.

Gamer, M., & Krook, A. K. (n.d.). *Job-interviewing handout.* Retrieved from http://www.english.upenn.edu/~mgamer/interview.html

Gaugler, J. E. (2004). On the tenure track in gerontology: I wish I had known then what I know now. *Educational Gerontology, 30,* 517–536. doi:10.1080/03601270490445122

Gerhart, B., & Rynes, S. (1991). Determinants and consequents of salary negotiations by male and female MBA graduates. *Journal of Applied Psychology, 76,* 256–262. doi:10.1037/0021-9010.76.2.256

Ginorio, A. B., Yee, B. W. K., Banks, M. E., & Todd-Bazemore, E. (2011). Surviving and thriving in academia. *American Psychological Association.* Retrieved from http://www.apa.org/pi/oema/resources/brochures/surviving.aspx#

Gmelch, H. W., & Miskin, V. D. (1995). *Chairing an academic department.* Thousand Oaks, CA: Sage.

Goldberg, C., & Cohen, D. J. (2004). Walking the walk and talking the talk: Gender differences in the impact of interviewing skills on applicant assessments. *Group & Organization Management, 29,* 369–384. doi:10.1177/1059601103257408

Graduate College Career Services Office, University of Illinois at Urbana-Champaign. (2006). *The nonacademic job search for graduate students.* Retrieved from http://www.grad.illinois.edu/careerservices/nonacademic/jobsearch/NonacJobSearchHandout.pdf

Grundman, H. G. (2006). Writing a teaching philosophy statement. *Notices of the American Mathematical Society, 53,* 1329–1333.

Hammer, E. D., & Yost Hammer, E. (2009). Maximizing your graduate training: Issues to think about from the start. In S. F. Davis, P. J. Giordano, & C. A. Licht (Eds.), *Your career in psychology: Putting your graduate degree to work* (pp. 3–12). Malden, MA: Wiley-Blackwell.

Haugen, L. (1998). Writing a teaching philosophy statement. *Iowa State University Center for Excellence in Learning and Teaching.* Retrieved from http://www.celt.iastate.edu/teaching/philosophy.html

Heiberger, M. M., & Vick, J. M. (1999, January 22). How to handle difficult interview questions. *The Chronicle of Higher Education.* Retrieved from http://chronicle.com/article/How-To-Handle-Difficult/45704

Hitchings, P., & Ornellas, J. (1999). Preparing for a job. In R. Bor & M. Watts (Eds.), *The trainee handbook: A guide for counseling and psychotherapy trainees* (pp. 268–285). London, England: Sage.

Hodges, S., & Connelly, A. R. (2010). *A job search manual for counselors and counselor educators.* Alexandria, VA: American Counseling Association.

Huang-Pollock, C. L., & Mikami, A. Y. (2007). The academic job search: Time line, tips, and tactics. *The Behavior Therapist, 30,* 104–108.

Humphrey, N. N., & Kang, E. (2009). The role of the psychologist in a medical setting: The interdisciplinary team approach. In S. F. Davis, P. J. Giordano, & C. A. Licht (Eds.), *Your career in psychology: Putting your graduate degree to work* (pp. 215–228). Malden, MA: Wiley-Blackwell.

Jackson, A. L., & Geckeis, C. K. (2003). *How to prepared your curriculum vitae* (Revised ed.). Chicago, IL: VGM Books/McGraw-Hill.

Jenkins, R. (2008, February 11). The community-college interview: What not to do. *The Chronicle of Higher Education.* Retrieved from http://chronicle.com/article/The-Community-College/45951/

Jenkins, R. (2010, October 11). That crucial first impression. *The Chronicle of Higher Education, 57*(8), A39–A41.

Johnson, M. D. (2004, October 15). The academic job interview revisited. *The Chronicle of Higher Education.* Retrieved from http://chronicle.com/article/The-Academic-Job-Interview-/44607/

Kaplan, M. (1998). The teaching portfolio. *CLRT Occasional Papers (no. 11).* Retrieved from http://www.crlt.umich.edu/publinks/CRLT_no11.pdf

Knouse, S. B., Giacalone, R. A., & Pollard, H. (1988). Impression management in the resume and its cover letter. *Journal of Business and Psychology, 3,* 242–249. doi:10.1007/BF01014492

Kuther, T. L. (2008). *Surviving graduate school in psychology: A pocket mentor.* Washington, DC: American Psychological Association.

Kuther, T. L. (2011). What to ask during and academic job interview. *About.com.* Retrieved from http://gradschool.about.com/cs/academic search/a/facint.htm

Landrum, R. E., & Clump, M. A. (2004). Departmental search committees and the evaluation of faculty applicants. *Teaching of Psychology, 31,* 12–17. doi:10.1207/s15328023top3101_4

Lang, J. M. (2010, September 3). 5 steps to a memorable teaching philosophy. *The Chronicle of Higher Education, 57,* A61, A63.

Levendusky, P. G. (1986). The clinical job interview: From the ivory tower to the real world. *The Behavior Therapist, 9,* 11–12.

Lopez, S. J., & Prosser, E. C. (2000). Becoming an adaptive new professional: Going beyond Plante's principles. *Professional Psychology: Research and Practice, 31,* 461–462. doi:10.1037/0735-7028.31.4.461

Madera, J. M., Hebl, M., & Martin, R. C. (2009). Gender and letters of recommendation for academia: Agentic and communal differences. *Journal of Applied Psychology, 94,* 1591–1599. doi:10.1037/a0016539

Mangum, T. (2009, August 19). Getting the letters right. *Inside Higher Ed.* Retrieved from http://www.insidehighered.com/advice/academic_career_confidential/mangum8?no_mobile_redirect=true

Marks, M., & Harold, C. (2011). Who asks and who receives in salary negotiation. *Journal of Organizational Behavior, 32,* 371–394. doi:10.1002/job.671

Matthews, J. R. (2000). Special issues facing new faculty with doctorates in applied subfields. *Teaching of Psychology, 27,* 216–217.

The McGraw Center for Teaching and Learning. (2010, October 27). *Writing teaching statements and philosophies.* Retrieved from http://www.princeton.edu/mcgraw/library/for-grad-students/teaching-statement/

Medina-Walpole, A., Fonzi, J., & Katz, P. R. (2007). Academic career development in geriatric fellowship training. *Journal of the American Geriatrics Society, 55,* 2061–2067. doi:10.1111/j.1532-5415.2007.01425.x

Meyers, S. A., Reid, P. T., & Quina, K. (1998). Ready or not, here we come: Preparing psychology graduate students for academic careers. *Teaching of Psychology, 25,* 124–126. doi:10.1207/s15328023top2502_11

Michalski, D., & Pate, W. (2010, August). *Funding issues and resources for clinically oriented graduate students.* Paper presented at the American Psychological Association annual convention, San Diego, CA.

Mielcarek, L., & Borbely, C. J. (2011). *The non-academic career path.* Washington, DC: American Psychological Association. Retrieved from http://www.apa.org/careers/resources/profiles/non-academic.aspx

Montell, G. (2001, March 16). Academic job searching for dummies (or, 10 easy ways to avoid unemployment). *The Chronicle of Higher Education.* Retrieved from http://chronicle.com/article/Academic-Job-Searching-for/45367/

Montell, G. (2003, March 27). What's your philosophy on teaching, and does it matter? *The Chronicle of Higher Education.* Retrieved from http://chronicle.com/article/Whats-Your-Philosophy-on/45132/

Mues, F., & Sorcinelli, M. D. (2000). *Preparing a teaching portfolio.* Retrieved from http://faculty.ksu.edu.sa/Mahmoud/DocLib8/preparing%20Teaching%20Portfolio.pdf

Mullins, M. E., & Rogers, C. (2008). Reliance on intuition and faculty hiring. *Industrial and Organizational Psychology: Perspectives on Science and Practice, 1,* 370–371. doi:10.1111/j.1754-9434.2008.00067.x

Mulvey, T. A., & Grus, C. L. (2010, August). *What can I do with a degree in psychology?* Paper presented at the American Psychological Association annual convention, San Diego, CA.

Newhouse, M. (1998, December 4). Transferring your skills to a non-academic setting. *The Chronicle of Higher Education*. Retrieved from http://chronicle.com/article/Transferring-Your-Skills-to-a/46430

Nicklin, J. M., & Roch, S. G. (2008). Biases influencing recommendation letter contents: Physical attractiveness and gender. *Journal of Applied Social Psychology, 38*, 3053–3074. doi:10.1111/j.1559-1816.2008.00425.x

Nowviskie, B. (2010, August, 31). The #alt-ac track: Negotiating your alternative academic appointment. *The Chronicle of Higher Education*. Retrieved from http://chronicle.com/blogs/profhacker/the-alt-ac-track-negotiating-your-alternative-academic-appointment-2/26539

O'Neal, C., Meizlish, D. S., & Kaplan, M.. (2007). Writing a statement of teaching philosophy for the academic job search. *CLRT Occasional Papers (no. 23)*. Retrieved from http://www.crlt.umich.edu/publinks/CRLT_no23.pdf

Plante, T. G. (1998). How to find a first job in professional psychology: Ten principles for finding employment for psychology interns and postdoctoral fellows. *Professional Psychology: Research and Practice, 29*, 508–511. doi:10.1037/0735-7028.29.5.508

Porter, C. O. L. H., Conlon, D. E., & Barber, A. E. (2004). The dynamics of salary negotiations: Effects on applicants' justice perceptions and recruitment decisions. *International Journal of Conflict Management, 15*, 273–303. doi:10.1108/eb022915

Potter, C. B. (2010, November 28). The job market is s lot like the PBS NewsHour, and other advice for Skype interviews. *Tenured Radical*. Retrieved from http://tenured-radical.blogspot.com/2010/11/why-job-market-is-lot-like-pbs-newshour.html

Preparing Future Faculty. (n.d.). *The Preparing Future Faculty program*. Retrieved from http://www.preparing-faculty.org/

Prinstein, M. J. (2007). The interview. In C. Williams-Nickelson & M. J. Prinstein (Eds.), *Internships in psychology: The APAGS workbook for writing successful applications and finding the right match* (pp. 79–92). Washington, DC: American Psychological Association.

Prinstein, M. J. (2008). The interview. In C. Williams-Nickelson, M. J. Prinstein, & W. G. Keilin (Eds.), *Internships in psychology: The APAGS workbook for writing successful applications and finding the right fit* (2nd ed., pp. 97–112). Washington, DC: American Psychological Association.

Purdue Online Writing Lab. (2011). *Writing the Curriculum Vitae*. Retrieved from http://owl.english.purdue.edu/owl/resource/641/01/

Range, L. M., Menyhert, A., Walsh, M. L., Hardin, K. N., Ellis, J. B., & Craddick, R. (1991). Letter of recommendation: Perspectives, recommendations, and ethics. *Professional Psychology: Research and Practice, 22*, 389–392. doi:10.1037/0735-7028.22.5.389

Reis, R. M. (2001, February 2). Getting great letters of recommendation. *The Chronicle of Higher Education Chronicle Careers*. Retrieved from http://grad-affairs.uchicago.edu/academic-resources/Getting%20Great%20Letters%20of%20Recommendation.pdf

Rodriguez-Farrar, H. B. (2008). *The teaching portfolio: A handbook for faculty, teaching assistants and teaching fellows*. Retrieved from http://brown.edu/Administration/Sheridan_Center/teaching/documents/TeachingPortfolio.pdf

Schall, J. (2006). The ethics of writing letters of recommendation. *Academe Online*. Retrieved from http://www.aaup.org/AAUP/pubsres/academe/2006/MJ/feat/scha.htm

Schwebel, D. C., & Karver, M. S. (2004). Recent trends in the research-oriented clinical psychology academic job market. *The Behavior Therapist, 27*, 174–179.

Seelig, T. (2010, February 15). Secrets to a successful job interview. *Psychology Today*. Retrieved from http://www.psychologytoday.com/blog/creativityrulz/201002/secrets-successful-job-interview

Sego, T., & Richards, J. I. (1995). *Ph.D. interview preparation guide for positions in academia*. Retrieved from http://www.unl.edu/postdoc/documents/interview_prep.pdf

Seldin, P. (1993). *Successful use of teaching portfolios*. Boston, MA: Anker.

Sha, R. C. (2011, January). Job letter mistakes. *Inside Higher Ed*. Retrieved from http://www.insidehighered.com/advice/2011/01/12/sha

Sheehan, E. P., & Haselhorst, H. (1999). A profile of applicants for an academic position in social psychology. *Journal of Social Behavior & Personality, 14*, 23–30.

Sheehan, E. P., McDevitt, T. M., & Ross, H. C. (1998). Looking for a job as a psychology professor? Factors affecting applicant success. *Teaching of Psychology, 25*, 8–11. doi:10.1207/s15328023top2501_3

Sies, M. C. (1996). *Academic job interview advice*. Retrieved from http://otal.umd.edu/~sies/jobadvice.html

Simmons, A. (2006). *The story factor: Inspiration, influence, and persuasion through the art of storytelling*. New York, NY: Basic Books.

Simpson, D. (2006). Preparing your curriculum vitae. In L. W. Roberts & D. Hilty (Eds.), *Handbook of career development in academic psychiatry and behavioral sciences* (pp. 49–60). Washington, DC: American Psychiatric Publishing.

Sinclair, R. (2006, August, 24). A dean's take on salary negotiation. *The Chronicle of Higher Education*. Retrieved from http://chronicle.com/article/A-Deans-Take-On-Salary/46747/

Skidmore College Career Services. (2011). *Evaluating job offers and negotiating salary*. Retrieved from http://cms.skidmore.edu/career/communications/handouts/upload/negotiating.pdf

SkillStorm. (2009). *How blogging and social networking can impact your job search.* Retrieved from: http://www.skillstorm.com/blog/?p=39

Small, D. A., Gelfand, M., Babcock, L., & Gettman, H. (2007). Who goes to the bargaining table? The influence of gender and framing on the initiation of negotiation. *Journal of Personality and Social Psychology, 93,* 600–613. doi:10.1037/0022-3514.93.4.600

Smallwood, S. (2001, January 12). Psychology Ph.D.'s pass on academe. *The Chronicle of Higher Education, 43,* A10–A12.

Smith, R. A. (2009). Being a good departmental citizen: Getting your career off on the right track. In S. F. Davis, P. J. Giordano, & C. A. Licht (Eds.), *Your career in psychology: Putting your graduate degree to work* (pp. 75–87). Malden, MA: Wiley-Blackwell.

Smith, S. L. (2007). *Writing a philosophy of teaching statement.* Retrieved from http://www.d.umn.edu/gk12/ePortfolio/2009-2010-GK12 Documents/WritingTeachingStatement2009-2010.doc

Smith, Z., & Sutton-Grier, A. (2010, July 15). Making the most of your post doc. *The Chronicle of Higher Education.* Retrieved from http://chronicle.com/article/Making-the-Most-of-Your/66265/

Snyder, T. D., & Dillow, S. A. (2011). *Digest of education statistics 2010* (NCES Report No. 2010-015, Table 326). Washington, DC: National Center for Education Statistics, Institute of Education Sciences, U.S. Department of Education.

Social Psychology Network. (2011). Advice on letters of recommendation. *Social Psychology Network.* Retrieved from http://www.socialpsychology.org/rectips.htm

Sowers-Hoag, K., & Harrison, D. F. (1998). *Finding an academic job.* Thousand Oaks, CA: Sage.

Stanford Career Development Center. (2004). *Dossier preparation: Teaching portfolios and teaching/research/personal statements.* Retrieved from http://studentaffairs.stanford.edu/sites/default/files/cdc/files/Dossier Preparation_05-06.pdf

Sternberg, R. J. (2003). The job search. In M. J. Prinstein & M. D. Patterson (Eds.), *The portable mentor: Expert guide to a successful career in psychology* (pp. 297–308). New York, NY: Kluwer.

Sternberg, R. J. (2004). Obtaining a research grant: The applicant's view. In J. M. Darley, M. P. Zanna, & H. L. Roediger, III, (Eds.), *The compleat academic: A career guide* (2nd ed., pp. 169–184). Washington, DC: American Psychological Association.

Sternberg, R. J. (2006). *Career paths in psychology: Where your degree can take you.* Washington, DC: American Psychological Association.

Sufka, K. J. (2009). Preparing for a career at a research university. In S. F. Davis, P. J. Giordano, & C. A. Licht (Eds.), *Your career in psychology: Putting your graduate degree to work* (pp. 103–115). Malden, MA: Wiley-Blackwell.

Thompson, K. (2009, Fall). Cover your bases with a savvy cover letter. *Phi Kappa Phi Forum, 89*(3), 25.

Thompson, K. & Wein, T. I. (2004, December 17). From CV to resume. *Chronicle of Higher Education*. Retrieved from http://chronicle.com/article/From-CV-to-R-sum-/44712

Ting, L. H. (2008). *Constructing your research statement*. Retrieved from http://www.neuro.gatech.edu/groups/ting/assets/pdf/Research-Statement.pdf

Trabb. (2007, August 10). Re: Surviving the job search [Online forum comment]. Retrieved from http://chronicle.com/forums/index.php?topic=40486.0

University of California, Berkeley, Career Center. (2009, May 20). *PhDs—Letters of recommendation*. Retrieved from https://career.berkeley.edu/Phds/PhDLetters.stm

University of California, Berkeley, Career Center. (2011, March 16). *PhDs—Teaching portfolio*. Retrieved from https://career.berkeley.edu/phds/PhDportfolio.stm

University Center for the Advancement of Teaching. (2009, November 12). *Writing a philosophy of teaching statement*. Retrieved from http://ucat.osu.edu/portfolio/philosophy/Philosophy.html

University of Nebraska—Lincoln. (2011, February). The academic job talk. *Graduate Connections*. Retrieved from http://www.unl.edu/gradstudies/current/dev/newsletter/GradConnections-201102.pdf

UTSA University Career Center. (2010). *Interviewing for research and teaching positions*. Retrieved from http://utsa.edu/careercenter/students/graduate_students/interviewing_research_teaching.html

Varma, A., Toh, S. M., & Pichler, S. (2006). Ingratiation in job applications: Impact on selection decisions. *Journal of Managerial Psychology, 21*, 200–210. doi:10.1108/02683940610659551

Vick, J. M., & Furlong, J. S. (2008, January 31). How to write a good recommendation. *The Chronicle of Higher Education*. Retrieved from http://chronicle.com/article/How-to-Write-a-Good/45944

Vick, J., & Heiberger, M. M. (2002, March 22). Negotiating a better deal. *The Chronicle of Higher Education*. Retrieved from http://chronicle.com/article/Negotiating-a-Better-Deal/45986/

Vincent, C. (2008, July 24). The rejection letter I wish I could send. *The Chronicle of Higher Education, 56*(17), D5–D6.

Wagner, R. (2000, December 8). The secret to a successful job interview. *Chronicle of Higher Education*. Retrieved from http://chronicle.com/article/The-Secret-to-a-Successful-Job/46366/

Weimer, M. (2010, August 20). *Preparing teaching philosophy statements*. Retrieved from http://www.facultyfocus.com/

Williams-Nickelson, C., & Prinstein, M. J. (2007). Supplementary materials. In C. Williams-Nickelson & M. J. Prinstein (Eds.), *Internships in psychology: The APAGS workbook for writing successful applications and finding the right match* (pp. 49–77). Washington, DC: American Psychological Association.

Willingham, D. T. (2009). *Why don't students like school?* San Francisco, CA: Jossey-Bass.

Woolf, E. (2010, October 13). Standing out from the herd. *Inside Higher Ed.* Retrieved from http://www.insidehighered.com/advice/on_the_fence/woolf7

Index

About the Authors

Elizabeth M. Morgan, PhD, is an assistant professor of psychology at Boise State University. She received her doctorate in developmental psychology from the University of California, Santa Cruz, in 2008. She also has a master's degree in social work from the University of Michigan. Her research focuses on adolescent and young adult social development, with an emphasis on sexual and romantic relationship experiences in the context of parent–child relationships, peer relationships, and the media. Boise State University is her first academic position, which she obtained directly after finishing her PhD. During the process of preparing and applying for faculty positions, she found herself relying on many different sources for information about how to compile an application and what to expect in her interviews; these sources she found to be inadequate. Also, as both a first- and second-year faculty member, she was able to be a part of Boise State's psychology department search committee, reviewing application materials, interviewing candidates by phone, checking references, and hosting candidates on campus. This book was conceived as a result of being on both ends of the process within the span of only a few years.

R. Eric Landrum, PhD, is a professor of psychology at Boise State University. He received his doctorate in cognitive psychology from Southern Illinois University at Carbondale. His research interests center on the educational conditions that best facilitate student success (broadly defined). He has given over 280 professional presentations at conferences and has published 17 books or book chapters and over 70 professional articles in scholarly, peer-reviewed journals. He has worked with over 275 undergraduate research assistants and taught over 12,500 students in 20 years at Boise State. During the summer of 2008, he led a working group at the National Conference for Undergraduate Education in Psychology, studying the desired results of an undergraduate psychology education.

Eric is the lead author of *The Psychology Major: Career Options and Strategies for Success* (4th ed., 2009) and also authored *Undergraduate Writing in Psychology: Learning to Tell the Scientific Story* (2008) and *Finding a Job With a Psychology Bachelor's Degree: Expert Advice for Launching Your Career* (2009). He is a member of the American Psychological Association (APA), Fellow of APA Division 2 (Society for the Teaching of Psychology), and served as Division 2 secretary. He teaches general psychology, statistical methods, research methods, psychological measurement, and a Capstone course on history and systems in psychology.